CONTEMPORARY
WORLD
GOLD COINS

1934 - 1974

CONTEMPORARY
WORLD
GOLD COINS

1934 - 1974
by Sanford J. Durst

Credits and Acknowledgements

Many sources from the world over went into the compilation of data for this book, including several fine catalogs previously published for use by collectors, price lists, sales brochures, auction catalogs, and news articles.

Of particular note as source material are "Gold Coins of the World" by Robert Friedberg, Third Edition; "World Coin Catalog-Twentieth Century" by Gunter Schon, English Edition; "Gold Munzen Katalog" Second Edition by Hans Schlumberger; "Standard Catalog of World Coins" by Chester L. Kraus and Clifford Mishler, Second Edition; "The Guidebook and Catalog of British Commonwealth Coins" Third Edition by Jerome Remick, Somer James, Anthony Dowle and Patrick Finn; "Gold Coins of the Americas" by Robert P. Harris; "Modern World Coins" Tenth Edition by R. S. Yeoman, and "Current Coins of the World" Fifth Edition by R. S. Yeoman; the fine sales catalogs of Spink & Son, Ltd. of London. Many of the photographs were provided by Italcambio of Miami, Florida.

TABLE OF CONTENTS

TABLE OF CONTENTS (cont.)

FORWARD

The change in U.S. law permitting Americans to own gold coins minted after 1933 has brought with it the need for an accurate and orderly catalogue containing this vital numismatic information. Sanford Durst's new book fills this need admirably.

Mr. Durst is a careful and conscientious numismatist who has painstakingly gathered his information wherever it was available. His research was made doubly difficult because the coins covered herein have not been available in the United States, necessitating the careful perusal of foreign offerings, European auction catalogues, mint notices and endless correspondence abroad in order to present an accurate portrayal of this material.

That Mr. Durst has succeeded in his quest is abundantly clear to the reader of these pages. Not only are all the listed coins fully described in detail as to weight, size, fineness and amount of issue, but most are photographed as well. Such a complete compendium is an absolute must in every numismatic library, and is particularly useful for those who expect to add these beautiful modern coins to their collections.

Especially useful is information that distinguishes coin-of-the-realm legitimate issues from the plethora of material minted quasi-privately, whose only real function is to ease the passage of bullion from country to country, while reaping the financial benefits of induced or built-in scarity!

It is expected that this catalogue will appear yearly, with all new issues included, and pricing brought up-to-date. This is good news for the collector who heretofore has had to depend on scattered foreign listings to fill the gap from 1933 to the present time. Mr. Durst has written a useful book, and the numismatic fraternity is grateful!

Joseph H. Rose
President, Harmer Rooke Numismatists, Ltd.

Introduction

Many long time gold coin collectors and those newly interested in the hobby have during the recent past been unable to buy modern gold coin rarities, while their counterparts in other areas did so to their pleasure (and obvious profit).

This catalog is presented to all collectors and dealers as a reference, to assist in collecting, purchasing, investing in this active area of Numismatics.

It has been designed to cover the 4 decades 1934-1974, specifically chosen as that period during which it was illegal for U.S. citizens to own gold in any form (with minor exceptions). Of course, coins minted after 1933 were specifically prohibited. Since December 17, 1973 the law was changed to permit ownership of coins dated from 1934-1959. But this opened only a limited access to purchase gold coins by U.S. collectors, since there were very few gold coins of that period. Hence 1934-1959 is worth including.

For some time I have anticipated this moment, in numismatic history and have carefully followed notices of foreign mints, price lists of European and Canadian dealers, European Auction catalogs, news items in numismatic papers, price lists of foreign banks, etc., resulting in an accumulation of a very substantial quantity of information on the coins which are the subject of this catalog. Included are retail prices currently being paid for these coins, mintages, sizes, weights, illustrations, and other pertinent data. The information has of course been put into logical sequence for maximum utility.

Substantially important to the collector after identification of a coin, is of course its current value and, in this area, great care has been taken to present the most up-to-date information possible. However it is expected that after the U.S. Market in modern gold coins opens in 1975, prices of some modern gold coins will rise dramatically. To further assist the collector, in this regard a NEWSLETTER service will be available specifically designed to keep the collector/investor up to date on new issues, price information, and other pertinent data. Information on this Newsletter is at the end of the catalog.

Coins which are scheduled for release as of the time of this writing, have been included as this is considered useful information for the collector. Coins which have been issued, with questionable status, such as so-called "coin-medals" and "non-circulating legal tender" have also been included, and are so identified by the symbols CM or NCLT.

Metals such as platinum and palladium have been used to produce contemporary coins, and they have been included, since gold-oriented numismatists also usually include these coins in their gold collections.

A word of caution: Because there will be unusually keen interest in purchasing contemporary gold coins, some counterfeiting has and will continue to take place. When you purchase, do it from a reputable dealer—someone who will stand behind the coins sold to you—with reasonable return privileges.

Happy Collecting!!

Sanford J. Durst

ON USING THIS CATALOG

This catalog is arranged alphabetically, country by country, with a table of contents at the beginning of the book.

Within each nation coins are arranged generally in chronological order, earlier years first. Each coin is numbered for reference purposes by collectors, dealers, and auctioneers, with denomination, year and current international market value as of November 1974, in U.S. dollars.

Sizes and mintages use the universally accepted (mm) millimeters and (gms) grams. Fineness is expressed in 1000 fine being pure gold (24 carat), for example 900 fine (the most common quality used in gold coins is 900/1000 or 90% pure gold). Mintages are actual numbers reported issued. Where large numbers of the coins were issued over many years, total mintages of these common type gold coins are given.

Special sections in the rear portion of the book cover important data for collectors such as conversion of weights and measures; intrinsic value of common bullion coins at different gold bullion prices; list of countries having announced issue of new gold coins; cross-reference of denominations and countries; the storage and care of gold coins.

Where information is unavailable or doubtful, blank spaces have been intentionally left, so the collector can fill in data, as he acquires it.

Where a coin is indicated as NCLT, this means "Non Circulating Legal Tender", coins manufactured exclusively for collectors, and not for circulation in the nation of issue.

ND means "no date". Photographs appear below listing in each instance.

Where "est." appears before a value, the market is either so thin, or no worthwhile data is available, and the author has estimated the market based on similar coins of like nations, mintages, gold content, and other experience factors.

Prices are based on either BU coins, or proof where indicated, since most modern gold coins have been held by collectors, who have carefully preserved them. The result, few are circulated, eliminating the current need for prices in say XF or VF (or lower grades).

AFGHANISTAN

1. ½ Dinar 1314 AH (1936 AD) $95
2. 1 Dinar 1314 AH (1936 AD) $130
3. 1 Amani 1313 AH (1935 AD) $180

Obv: Throne Room Scene. Rev: Inscription surrounded by Wreath. Issued by Zahir Shah, in power since 1933.

Sizes and weights:
½ Dinar,   mm, 4 gms 900 fine
1 Dinar, 19 mm, 8 gms 900 fine
1 Amani, 19 mm, 4.55 gms 900 fine
Mintages:

AJMAN

1. 100 Riyals (Lenin) $200
2. 50 Riyals (Nasser) $80
3. 25 Riyals (Martin Luther King) $50
4. 25 Riyals (George Marshall) $50
5. 25 Riyals (Mahatma Ghandi) $50
6. 25 Riyals (Jan Palach) $50
7. 25 Riyals (Albert Schweitzer) $50
8. 25 Riyals (Bertrand Russell) $50
9. 25 Riyals (Dag Hammarskjold) $50
10. 25 Riyals (Albert Luthuli) $50
11. 25 Riyals (Nasser) $50
12. 25 Riyals (Save Venice) $50
13. 50 Riyals (Save Venice) $80
14. 100 Riyals (Save Venice) $200
15. 75 Riyals (Fish) $150

Obv: #1-11 have Busts of Named Individuals. All are proofs and are considered NCLT.

Sizes and weights:
25 Riyals, 21 mm, 5.17 gms 900 fine
50 Riyals, 24 mm, 10.35 gms 900 fine
75 Riyals, 28 mm, 15.53 gms 900 fine
100 Riyals, 31 mm, 20.7 gms 900 fine

Mintages: *
25 Riyals—(Nasser)—1100; 25 Riyals—1750 each; 50 Riyals—(Nasser)—700; 100 Riyals—(Lenin)—1000; Venice Set—
75 Riyals—
*Unconfirmed

ALBANIA

1. 20 Francs 1937 .... $300
2. 100 Francs 1937 .... $950

Issued to commemorate 25th Anniversary of Independence. Obv: Zog I. Rev: Coat of Arms.

3. 20 Francs 1938 .... $350
4. 100 Francs 1938 .... $2500

Issued to commemorate wedding of King, April 27, 1938. Obv: Zog I. Rev: Coat of Arms and date 27 IV 1938.

5. 20 Francs 1938 .... $300
6. 50 Francs 1938 .... $1300
7. 100 Francs 1938 .... $2500

Issued to commemorate 10th year of King's Rule. Obv: Zog I. Rev: Coat of Arms and dates I • IX • 1928 • 1938.

ALBANIA (cont.)

8. **20 Leks 1968** $45
9. **50 Leks 1968** $85
10. **100 Leks 1968** $185
11. **200 Leks 1968** $300
12. **500 Leks 1968** $850

Rev: Coat of Arms. Obv: 20 Lek, Helmet & Sword Surrounded by Wreath; 50 Leks, Viaduct and Fort; 100 Leks, Girl Picking Fruit; 200 Leks, Head of Woman; 500 Leks, Bust of Skanderbeg. Considered NCLT. All are proofs. There are 3 silver companion pieces.

Rev.

Mintages:
20 Francs 1937,8–2500 each year; 100 Francs 1937,8–500 each year; #5–20 Francs 1938–1000; #6–50 Francs 1938–600; #7–100 Francs 1938–500; 20 Leks–200,000 max.; 50 Leks–160,000 max.; 100 Leks–100,000 max.; 200 Leks–80,000 max.; 500 Leks–12,000 max.

ANGUILLA

1. **5 Dollars 1967** $35
2. **10 Dollars 1967** $65
3. **20 Dollars 1967** $110
4. **100 Dollars 1967** $450
5. **50 Peso Counterstamp 1967** . . . . **Rare**

Rev: Coat of Arms. Obv: as follows: $5 Scene of Church; $10 Underwater; $20 Two Mermaids; $100 Circle of People. 50 Peso–The Mexican 50 Peso Gold 1.2 oz gold 900 fine. A presentation piece counterstamped "100 Liberty Dollars". There are 4 silver proof companion pieces. These coins are all proof and considered NCLT.

Sizes and weights:
20 Francs, 20 mm, 6.45 gms 900 fine
50 Francs,   mm, 16.12 gms 900 fine
100 Francs, 33 mm, 32.25 gms 900 fine
20 Leks, 21 mm, 3.95 gms 900 fine
50 Leks, 26 mm, 9.87 gms 900 fine
100 Leks, 32 mm, 19.75 gms 900 fine
200 Leks, 45 mm, 39.49 gms 900 fine
500 Leks, 55 mm, 98.74 gms 900 fine

ANGUILLA (cont.)

Rev.

Sizes and weights:
$5, 15 mm, 2.46 gms 900 fine
$10, 18 mm, 4.93 gms 900 fine
$20, 23 mm, 9.87 gms 900 fine
$100, 50 mm, 49.37 gms 900 fine

Mintages:
$5 thru $100—10,000 sets; 50 Peso—2 pieces.

AUSTRIA

1. 25 Schillings 1934 . . . . **$120**
2. 100 Schillings 1934 . . . . **$500**

Obv: Eagle. Rev: Value and Date between Branches. Last year of a continuing series from 1926.

3. 100 Schillings 1935-8 . . . . **$1250**

Obv: Standing Figure of Maria Zell Madonna. Rev: Austrian Imperial Eagle. The 1938 is extremely rare as most melted.

4. 25 Schillings 1935-8 . . . . **$450**

Obv: St. Leopold Holding Church. Rev: Austrian Imperial Eagle. The 1938 is extremely rare (only 10-12 pieces), as most ordered melted by occupation authorities. Sold for $4900, Hans Schulman auction, Oct. 15, 1974, New York.

Sizes and weights:
25 Shillings, 20 mm, 5.88 gms 900 fine
100 Shillings, 33 mm, 23.52 gms 900 fine

Mintages:
25 Shillings: 1934—9383; 1935—2880; 1936—7267; 1937—7665; 1938—1357.
100 Shillings: 1934—9383; 1935—951; 1936—12,417; 1937—2936; 1938—1433.

Note: The Austrian State Mint has been restriking gold coins as a business for several years. These coins are "bullion" coins issued for the purpose of profit for the mint and have been sold at 8-15% over bullion value, worldwide. Caution is advised in purchasing the coins dated as listed in the restrike section at the back of this catalog which in almost all cases are restrikes. (The originals and the restrikes cannot be told from one another.)

BAHAMAS
(Commonwealth of)

First Series:
1. 10 Dollars 1967 . . . . .proof set
2. 20 Dollars 1967 . . . .$1350
3. 50 Dollars 1967 . . . . .unc set
4. 100 Dollars 1967 . . . .$850

Obv: Bust of Queen Elizabeth II of Great Britain. Rev: $10, Fort; $20, Lighthouse; $50, The Santa Maria, the Flagship of Colombus; $100, Colombus Landing at San Salvador.

Obv.

Second Series:
5. 10 Dollars 1971 . . . . .unc set
6. 20 Dollars 1971 . . . .$700
7. 50 Dollars 1971 . . . . .proof set
8. 100 Dollars 1971 . . . .$900

Same description as First Series.

Third Series:
9. 10 Dollars 1972 . . . . .unc set
10. 20 Dollars 1972 . . . .$575
11. 50 Dollars 1972 . . . . .proof set
12. 10 Dollars 1972 . . . .$700

Same description as First Series.

Fourth Series:
13. 10 Dollars 1973 . . . . .Issue price:
14. 20 Dollars 1973 . . . .$400
15. 50 Dollars 1973 . . . . .proof set
16. 100 Dollars 1973 . . . . .unc set $240

Obv: Bust of Queen Elizabeth II of Great Britain. Rev: $10, Bird; $20, 4 Flamingos; $50, Lobster; $100, Coat of Arms. Issued in Red Gold and Yellow Gold.

Obv.

BAHAMAS (cont.)

17. $50 1973 (Flamingo) . . . . . . proof **$150**
                             unc **$120**

Obv: Bust of Queen Elizabeth II of Great Britain. Rev: Two Flamingos and Rising Sun.

Sizes and weights:
First and Second Series:
$10, 20 mm, 3.99 gms 916$^{2/3}$ fine
$20, 22 mm, 7.98 gms 916$^{2/3}$ fine
$50, 28 mm, 19.94 gms 916$^{2/3}$ fine
$100, 36 mm, 39.94 gms 916$^{2/3}$ fine

Third Series:
In 1972 the weights were reduced as follows: $10–3.19 gms; $20, 6.38 gms; $50, 15.97 gms and $100, 31.95 gms, with size and fineness the same as first and second series.

Fourth Series:
$10, 15 mm, 1.45 gms 585 fine
$20, 19 mm, 2.9 gms 585 fine
$50, 22 mm, 7.27 gms 585 fine
$100, 28 mm, 14.54 gms 585 fine
$50 Flamingo (1973), 29 mm, 15.5 gms 500 fine

Mintages:
1967 Series—proofs, 850 sets; unc, 1200 sets plus 2950 additional $10 and $20 pieces.
1971 Series—proofs, 1250 sets; unc,   sets.
1972 Series—proofs, 1250 sets; uncs, 2250 sets; $10 & 20, 12,000 mini-sets.
1973 Series—proofs, 1250 sets; uncs,   sets.
$50 Flamingo 1973 proofs, 17,593, unc, 22,000.

Announced: A series in 1974 and in 1975, similar to the prior annual coin series issued.

BAHRAIN

1. 10 Dinars 1968 . . . . **$225**

Issued to commemorate establishment of Town of Isa. Obv: Bust of Isa—Bin Sulman. Rev: Coat of Arms. There is a companion silver crown issued in the denomination of 500 fils.

Size and weight:
10 Dinars, 28 mm, 15.85 gms 916$^{2/3}$ fine

Mintage:
3000

BELIZE
(Formerly British Honduras)

Announced: For 1975, a $100 gold coin and $25 silver companion crown to commemorate the 100th Anniversary of the Birth of Winston Churchill.

BERMUDA

1. 20 Dollars 1970 . . . . **$650**

Obv: Bust of Queen Elizabeth II of Great Britain. Rev: Flying Bird. Issued as part of a proof set of coins. Very scarce.

BERMUDA (cont.)

Size and weight:*
20 Dollars, 22.5 mm, 8 gms 916²/₃ fine

*Weight unconfirmed

Mintage:
1000

BHUTAN

1. 1 Sertum 1966 . . . .$800 for unc
2. 2 Sertum 1966 . . . . set; $900 for
3. 5 Sertum 1966 . . . . proofset
4. 1 Sertum Platinum 1966 . . . . Rare
5. 5 Sertum Platinum 1966 . . . . Rare

Obv: Bust of Maharaja Jigme Wangchuk. Rev: Buddist Wheel of Life with Thunderbolt.

6. 1 Sertum 1970 . . . . $95

Obv: Bust of Girl. Rev: Emblem with Circular Description Around Edge.

Sizes and weights:
1 Sertum, 22 mm, 8 gms 916²/₃ fine
2 Sertum,   mm, 16 gms 916²/₃ fine
5 Sertum,   mm, 40 gms 916²/₃ fine
1 Sertum Platinum,   mm,   gms
5 Sertum Platinum,   mm,   gms

Mintages:
1 Sertum—proof—500, unc—2800; 2 Sertum—proof—500, unc—800; 5 Sertum—proof—500, unc—800. 1 Sertum—1970—5000. Platinum series: 100 each.

BIAFRA

1. 1 Pound 1959 . . . .
2. 2 Pounds 1969 . . . .$1100
3. 5 Pounds 1969 . . . . for
4. 10 Pounds 1969 . . . . the
5. 25 Pounds 1969 . . . . set.

Issued to commemorate 2nd Anniversary of Independence. Obv: Coat of Arms and Date. Rev: Eagle within Wreath and the Legend "The Fight For Survival". Price: Oct. 1974, original agent for the Nation.

BIAFRA (cont.)

Sizes and weights:
1 Pound, 17 mm, 3.99 gms 916⅔ fine
2 Pounds, 19.5 mm, 7.98 gms 916⅔ fine
5 Pounds, 24.5 mm, 15.97 gms 916⅔ fine
10 Pounds, 34 mm, 39.94 gms 916⅔ fine
25 Pounds, 44 mm, 79.88 gms 916⅔ fine

Mintage:
3000 sets.

BOLIVIA

1. 3½ gms 1952 . . . . $95
2. 7 gms 1952 . . . . $135
3. 14 gms 1952 . . . . $195
4. 35 gms 1952 . . . . $800

In 1952 this special issue was minted to commemorate the revolt of October 31, 1952. Obv: 3½ gms, Head of Worker; 7 gms, Bust of Miner; 14 gms, Head of Busch; 35 gms, Head of Villaroel. Rev: Coat of Arms. Because these coins were issued in weight rather than denomination, there has been some numismatic discussions as to whether they are coins or coin-medals. Generally today accepted as coins.

Rev.

Sizes and weights:
3½ gms, 17 mm, 3.8 gms 900 fine
7 gms, 23.5 mm, 7.7 gms 900 fine
14 gms, 28.5 mm, 15.5 gms 900 fine
35 gms, 37 mm, 38.9 gms 900 fine

Mintages:
3½ gms—28,568; 7 gms—78,571; 14 gms—7,142
35 gms—2,857.

BOTSWANA

1. 10 Thebes 1966 . . . . $110

Obv: Bust of Seretse Khama, President. Rev: Coat of Arms and Legend.

Size and weight:
10 Thebes, 25 mm, 11.3 gms 900 fine

Mintage:
5000

BRAZIL

. **Kubicshek 14.64 gms 1960** $110

)bv: Head of Kubicshek. Rev: Symbolic)esign, Date and Word "Brasilia." This is a oin-medal, issued to honor the former president of Brazil. It is prooflike and generally has een appearing in collections of foreign gold utside of the U.S. Therefore considered a umismatic item and included here. Also issued n 7.3 gm size.

. **300 Cruzeiros 1973** . . . . .Proof $275
BU $175

ssued to commemorate the 150th Anniversary f the Republic of Brazil. Obv: 2 Faces and)esign; Rev: Map of Brazil and Denomination. here are 2 companion pieces, one Aluminum 1 :ruzeiro and one Silver 20 Cruzeiro pieces. All 3 sued in prooflike condition at $90 US by }ank of Brazil. The gold piece has been sold ut as of August 1974.

Sizes and weights:
.ubicshek, 22 mm, 15.35 gms 900 fine
)0 Cruzeiros, 26 mm, 16.58 gms 900 fine

Mintages: *
ubicshek—   ; 300 Cruzeiros proof—900;
U—50,000.
Mintages unconfirmed.

BULGARIA

1. **10 Leva 1963** $100
2. **20 Leva 1963** $200

Issued to commemorate 1100th Anniversary of Cyrillic Alphabet in proof. Obv: Standing Sts. Cyril and Methodius. Rev: Value and Shield. Two companion silver pieces exist.

3. **10 Leva 1964** $100
4. **20 Leva 1964** $200

Issued to commemorate 20th Anniversary of Peoples Republic in proof. Obv: Premier Dimitrov. Rev: Value and Flag. Two companion silver pieces exist.

Sizes and weights:
10 Leva, 22 mm, 8.44 gms 900 fine
20 Leva, 27 mm, 16.88 gms 900 fine

Mintages:
10 Leva 1963—7,000; 20 Leva 1963—3,000; 10 Leva 1964—10,000; 20 Leva 1964—5,000.

BURMA

1. 1 Rupee $30
2. 2 Rupee $50
3. 4 Rupee $80

Obv: Peacock. Rev: Inscription.

Sizes and weights:
1 Rupee,　mm, 1 gms 900 fine
2 Rupee,　mm, 2 gms 900 fine
4 Rupee,　mm, 4 gms 900 fine

Mintages:

Note: Insurgents 2 gram coin in 1974, mintage unknown, 12 mm with peacock on one side and legend on the other. The coin has been available in the $25-30 range.

BURUNDI

1. 10 Francs 1962 .... .est.
2. 25 Francs 1962 .... $675
3. 50 Francs 1962 .... for the
4. 100 Francs 1962 .... set

Issued to commemorate Independence. Obv: Bust in Uniform of King Mwambustsa IV. Rev: Coat of Arms. All in proof. Considered NCLT.

5. 10 Francs 1965 .... est.
6. 25 Francs 1965 .... $675
7. 50 Francs 1965 .... for the
8. 100 Francs 1965 .... set

Obv: Bust of King Mwambustsa IV. Rev: Lions

Head in Shield Coat of Arms. All in proof. Considered NCLT.

Sizes and weights:
1962 Series:
10 Francs, 19 mm, 3.2 gms 900 fine
25 Francs, 21.5 mm, 8 gms 900 fine
50 Francs, 28 mm, 16 gms 900 fine
100 Francs, 34.5 mm, 32 gms 900 fine

1965 Series:
10 Francs, 21.5 mm, 3 gms 900 fine
25 Francs, 21.5 mm, 7.5 gms 900 fine
50 Francs, 28 mm, 15 gms 900 fine
100 Francs, 34.5 mm, 30 gms 900 fine

Mintages:
1962 Series—2500 plus 5000 additional 10 Franc pieces.
1965 Series—5000 each.

CAMBODIA

Announced: A 50,000 and a 100,000 Riel coin for 1975. Two companion silver pieces. The gold to be .900 fine and 7,000 sets are planned to be issued in proof and uncirculated. Designs unannounced.

CAMEROON
(Federal Republic of)

1. 1000 Francs 1970 .... $50
2. 3000 Francs 1970 .... $125
3. 5000 Francs 1970 .... $225
4. 10,000 Francs 1970 .... $450
5. 20,000 Francs 1970 .... $850

CAMEROON (cont.)

Issued to commemorate the 10th Anniversary of Independence. Obv: Bust of El Hadj Ahmadou Ahidjo. Rev: 1000 Franc, Design; 3000 Franc, Elk Horns; 5000 Franc, Seal of Nation; 10,000 Franc, Two Elk; 20,000 Franc, Coat of Arms. Issue is proof. Considered NCLT.

Obv.

Sizes and weights:
1000 Francs, 18 mm, 3.5 gms 900 fine
3000 Francs, 20.5 mm, 10.5 gms 900 fine
5000 Francs, 24 mm, 17.5 gms 900 fine
10,000 Francs, 30 mm, 35 gms 900 fine
20,000 Francs, 39 mm, 70 gms 900 fine

Mintage:
4000 numbered sets.

CANADA

1. 20 Dollars 1967 . . . . **$275**

Issued to commemorate 100th Anniversary of the Confederation of Canada. Proof only. A companion set of commemorative coins in 1, 5, 10, 25, 50 cents and One Dollar (silver) was issued. The entire set in leather presentation case is valued at $300. Obv: Head of Queen Elizabeth II of Great Britain. Rev: Coat of Arms.

The seal appearing on the $20 Centennial piece is not really the Coat of Arms of Canada but rather a hybrid of symbols representing various aspects of Canadian history. It "shows a shield supported by a lion and a unicorn holding the British and French standards, displays the emblem of Canada and the arms of the four countries from which her population has mainly come. In the upper left quarter of the shield are the three lions of England, upper right the Scottish lion. On the left is the harp of Ireland and on the right the three fleurs-de-lis of France. In the base are the maple leaves of modern Canada."

Size and weight:
20 Dollars, 27 mm, 18.27 gms 900 fine

Mintage:
337,512

CAYMAN ISLANDS

1. 25 Dollars 1972 ....proof $140
UNC $120

Issued to commemorate the 25th Anniversary of the Marriage of Queen Elizabeth II of Great Britain & Prince Phillip. Obv: Cojoined Heads of Elizabeth and Phillip. Rev: Coat of Arms, Date. Companion $25 Silver piece minted in unc & proof.

Size and weight:
25 Dollars, 27.1 mm, 13.6 gms 500 fine

Mintages:
Proof—4,000 (estimated); UNC—20,578.

Announced: A $100 gold coin in 1975 to commemorate the 100th Anniversary of the Birth of Winston Churchill. Also a $25 silver companion piece.

CENTRAL AFRICAN REPUBLIC

1. 1000 Francs 1970 ....$75
2. 3000 Francs 1970 ....$125
3. 5000 Francs 1970 ....$225
4. 10,000 Francs 1970 ....$450
5. 20,000 Francs 1970 ....$850

Obv: Bust of Jean Bodel Bokassa. Rev: 1000 Francs, Coat of Arms; 3000 Francs, Bust of Martin Luther King; 5000 Francs, Olympic Wrestlers; 10,000 Francs, 3 Female Heads and UN Symbol; 20,000 Francs, Food of the Republic, Issued in proof. These coins are considered NCLT.

Obv.

14

CENTRAL AFRICAN REPUBLIC (cont.)

Size and weight:
50 Peso, 36 mm, 20 gms 900 fine.

Mintage:
1500*

*Unconfirmed

Sizes and weights:
1000 Francs, 17 mm, 3.5 gms 900 fine
3000 Francs, 22 mm, 10.5 gms 900 fine
5000 Francs, 29 mm, 17.5 gms 900 fine
10,000 Francs, 35 mm, 35 gms 900 fine
20,000 Francs, 47 mm, 70 gms 900 fine

Mintage:
4000 numbered sets.

CENTRAL AMERICAN UNION (HONDURAS)

1. 50 Peso 1970 . . . .$200

In 1970 this 50 Peso coin-medal was issued by the Union of Central American Banks to commemorate their meeting in Honduras. Some rumor has it that the coins are used for inter-bank transfers of funds, but this is unconfirmed. The piece is proof with frosted devices. It is a numismatic collectible and is therefore included here. Obv: Tree and Legend. Rev: 5 Mountains and Sun, with Legend.

CHAD

1. 1000 Francs 1970 . . . .$75
2. 3000 Francs 1970 . . . .$110
3. 5000 Francs 1970 . . . .$140
4. 10,000 Francs 1970 . . . .$250
5. 20,000 Francs 1970 . . . .$475

Issued to commemorate the 10th Anniversary of Independence. Obv: 1000 Francs Head of Commandant Lamy. Rev: Nude Girls and Arms; 3000 Francs. Obv: Head of Gov. Eboue. Rev: Maps and Arms; 5000 Francs. Obv: Head of General Lelerc. Rev: Palm Trees, Buildings and Arms; 10,000 Francs Bust of General DeGaulle. Rev: Cross of Lorraine & Arms; 20,000 Francs. Obv: Head of President Tombalbaye. Rev: Agricultural Symbols. All proofs. Considered NCLT.

CHAD (cont.)

Sizes and weights:
1000 Francs, 18 mm, 3.5 gms 900 fine
3000 Francs, 27.5 mm, 17.5 gms 900 fine
5000 Francs, 32 mm, 17.5 gms 900 fine
10,000 Francs, 43 mm, 35 gms 900 fine
20,000 Francs, 52 mm, 70 gms 900 fine

Mintage:
4000 numbered sets.

CHILE

1. 20 Peso 1958-61	$60
2. 50 Peso 1958-62	$100
3. 100 Peso (10 Condores) 1934-58	$150
4. 50 Peso 1967 proof	$85
5. 100 Peso 1967 proof	$200
6. 200 Peso 1967 proof	$375
7. 500 Peso 1967 proof	$650

Nos. 1, 2, 3 similar to coins of 1926 series and thereafter. Obv: Liberty Head with Coiled Hair. Rev: Coat of Arms and 2 Values. Considered a bullion coin. The 1967 series is generally considered NCLT. Rev: Coat of Arms. Obv: 50 Peso, Bust of O'Higgins; 100 Peso, Liberty Head and Coin Machine; 200 Peso, O'Higgins and San Martin on Horseback; 500 Peso, Liberty Head and Flag.

CHILE (cont.)

Rev.

Sizes and weights:
20 Peso 1958-61, 18.5 mm 4.06 gms 900 fine
50 Peso 1958-62, 24.5 mm 10.16 gms 900 fine
100 Peso (10 Condores), 31 mm, 20.33 gms
   900 fine
50 Peso, 26 mm, 10.16 gms 900 fine
100 Peso, 30 mm, 20.33 gms 900 fine
200 Peso, 40 mm, 40.67 gms 900 fine
500 Peso, 50 mm, 101.69 gms 900 fine .

Mintage:
20 Peso 1958-61, Total 45,000; 50 Peso
1958-62, Total 60,000; 100 Peso (10 Condores)
Total (1934-58)—3,767,500; 1967 Series—
2,000 sets.

CHINA, REPUBLIC OF (NATIONALIST)

1. **1000 Yuan 1965** **$375**
2. **2000 Yuan 1965** **$700**

Issued to commemorate 100th Anniversary of birth of Dr. Sun Yat Sen. Obv: Head of Dr. Sun Yat Sen. Rev: Floral Wreath with Denomination.

3. **2000 Yuan 1966** **$700**

Issued to commemorate 80th Birthday of Chang Kai-Shek. Obv: Head of Chang Kai-Shek. Rev: Flowers and 2 Cranes.

Sizes and weights:
1000 Yuan, 25 mm, 14 gms 900 fine
2000 Yuan, 33.3 mm, 28 gms 900 fine

Mintages:*
1000 Yuan 1965—2000; 2000 Yuan
1965—2000; 2000 Yuan 1966—2000

*Unconfirmed

17

COLOMBIA

1. 100 Peso 1968 . . . . $65
2. 200 Peso 1968 . . . . $130
3. 300 Peso 1968 . . . . $200
4. 500 Peso 1968 . . . . $300
5. 1500 Peso 1968 . . . . $800

Issued to Commemorate the 39th International
Eucharistic Congress in Bogota. Obv: Head of
Pope Paul VI. Rev: Coat of Arms and Denom-
ination. All proof. Considered NCLT.

6. 100 Peso 1969 . . . . $65
7. 200 Peso 1969 . . . . $130
8. 300 Peso 1969 . . . . $200
9. 500 Peso 1969 . . . . $300
10. 1500 Peso 1968 . . . . $800

Honoring hero's of the Republic. Obv: Bust of
Simon Bolivar. Rev: 100 Peso, Bust of Paris;
200 Peso, Bust of Soublette; 300 Peso, Bust of
Anzoatequi; 500 Peso, Bust of Rondon; 1500
Peso, Bust of Santander. All proofs. Considered
NCLT.

11. 100 Peso 1971 . . . . $65
12. 200 Peso 1971 . . . . $130
13. 300 Peso 1971 . . . . $200
14. 500 Peso 1971 . . . . $300
15. 1500 Peso 1971 . . . . $800

Issued to commemorate the 6th Pan American
Games. Rev: Symbol of the Games. Obv: 100
Peso, Javelin Thrower; 200 Peso, Runner; 300
Peso,   ; 500 Peso, Woman & Child; 1500
Peso, Scene. All proofs. Considered NCLT.

16. 1500 Peso 1973 . . . . $22

Issued to commemorate the 50th Anniversar
of the Central Bank of Colombia. Obv: Pr
Colombian Jug, dates 1923-1973. Rev: Denom
ination. In large numbers and written out.

17. 1000 Peso 1973 . . . .
18. 1500 Peso 1973 . . . .$400 fo
19. 2000 Peso 1973 . . . . .the set

Issued to commemorate the 100th Anniversar
of the Birth of Guillermo Valencia. Obv: Bu
of Valencia. Rev: Coat of Arms, Denominatio
and Date. All proofs.

COLOMBIA (cont.)

Sizes and weights:
00 Peso, 20 mm, 4.3 gms 900 fine
00 Peso, 24 mm, 8.6 gms 900 fine
00 Peso, 28 mm, 12.9 gms 900 fine
00 Peso, 35 mm, 21.4 gms 900 fine
500 Peso, 50 mm, 64.5 gms 900 fine
500 Peso (1973 urn), 27 mm, 18.98 gms 900 fine
000 Peso 1973, 20 mm, 4.37 gms 900 fine
500 Peso 1973, 23.5 mm, 8.5 gms 900 fine
000 Peso 1973, 27 mm, 12.8 gms 900 fine

Mintages:
00 Peso 1968—27,887; 200 Peso
968—26,706; 300 Peso 1968—24,206; 500
eso 1968—12,206; 1500 Peso 1968—8806.

he 1968 Series issued as follows: 8000 com-
ete sets, balance of coins sold individually.
969 Series—6000 sets; 1971 Series—6000 sets;
973—1500 Peso (Urn)—5000; 1973 Series—
00 Peso—10,000; 1500 Peso—5000; 2000
eso—5000.

CONGO

. **10 Francs 1965** . . . .
. **20 Francs 1965** $650
. **25 Francs 1965** . . . . for
. **50 Francs 1965** . . . . the
. **100 Francs 1965** . . . . set

sued to commemorate the 5th Anniversary of
ndependence. Obv: Military Bust of President
oseph Kasavubu. Rev: 10 Francs and 20
rancs, Palm Trees; 25 Francs, 50 Francs and
00 Francs, Elephant. All proofs. Considered
CLT.

Sizes and weights:
10 Francs,   mm,   gms 900 fine
20 Francs,   mm,   gms 900 fine
25 Francs,   mm,   gms 900 fine
50 Francs,   mm,   gms 900 fine
100 Francs,   mm,   gms 900 fine

Mintage:
3000 numbered sets of which 70% reportedly
were melted.

COOK ISLANDS

Announced: A $100 gold coin commemorating
the 100th Anniversary of the Birth of Winston
Churchill in 1974-5. Also a $50 silver (58 mm)
companion silver piece. A $50 silver gold-plated
coin is also being offered as part of the series,
at $225, with 2500 coins to be minted.

COSTA RICA

1. **50 Colones 1970** $70
2. **100 Colones 1970** $140
3. **200 Colones 1970** $275
4. **500 Colones 1970** $700
5. **1000 Colones 1970** $1300

Obv: 50 Colones, Figure on Globe; 100 Colones, Native Art; 200 Colones Juan Santamaria
and Cannon; 500 Colones, Bust of Jesus Jimenez;
1000 Colones, Map, Sun, Waves and Mountains.
Rev: Coat of Arms. All proof. Considered
NCLT. Five silver companion coins.

Rev.

Sizes and weights:
50 Colones, 23 mm, 7.45 gms 900 fine
100 Colones, 30 mm, 14.9 gms 900 fine
200 Colones, 40 mm, 29.8 gms 900 fine
500 Colones, 55 mm, 74.52 gms 900 fine
1000 Colones, 60 mm, 149.04 gms 900 fine

Mintages:
3000 of each

Announced: 1500 Colones, part of Conserva
tion coin series. Obv: Coat of Arms. Rev: The
Great Anteater. 34 mm, 33.4 gms, 900 fine.
Issue of 10,000 unc and 3000 proofs. Two
silver companion pieces.

CROATIA

1. 500 Kuna 1941 . . . . **$3500**

Obv: Head of Duke of Aosta as King. Rev: Value & Shield. Not placed in circulation.

2. 500 Kuna 1943 (Fantasy) . . . . . **est. $750**

Obv: "50 Kuna 1934". Rev: Shield and Legend. Struck by Separatist Party. Rarely available or listed. Sold at Globus II auction for $575 in BU. Offered by one dealer in 1974 $400. Sold at Hans Schulman auction Oct. 15, 1974, New York for $750.

Sizes and weights:
500 Kuna (1941), 25 mm, 9.75 gms 900 fine
500 Kuna (1943), 25 mm, 11.79 gms 900 fine

Mintages:
500 kuna (1941)—140*; 500 Kuna (1943)— unknown, but rarely seen.

*Unconfirmed

CZECHOSLOVAKIA

1. 1 Ducat 1934-39, 51 . . . . $250
2. 2 Ducat 1934-38, 51 . . . . $500
3. 5 Ducat 1934-38, 51 . . . . $600
4. 10 Ducat 1934-38, 51 . . . . $1400

Obv: 1 and 2 Ducat, St. Wenzal; 5 and 10 Ducat, St. Wenzal on Horse. Rev: Coat of Arms and year.

5. 1 Ducat 1934 . . . . $500
6. 2 Ducat 1934 . . . . $500
7. 5 Ducat 1934 . . . . $1800
8. 10 Ducat 1934 . . . . $3500

Issued to commemorate reopening of the Kremnica Mines. Obv: St. Elizabeth in Prayer. Rev: Mining Scenes.

CZECHOSLOVAKIA (cont.)

Sizes and weights:
1 Ducat, 19.5 mm, 3.5 gms 986 fine
2 Ducat, 25 mm, 7.0 gms 986 fine
5 Ducat, 30 mm, 17.5 gms 986 fine
10 Ducat, 41 mm, 35 gms 986 fine

Mintages:
1 Ducat 1934—9729; 1935—13,178;
1936—14,566; 1937—324; 1938—56; 1939—20;
1951—500; 2 Ducat 1934—2403; 1935—2577;
1936—819; 1937—8; 1938—14; 1951—200; 5
Ducat 1934—1101; 1935—1037; 1936—728;
1937—4; 1938—12; 1951—100; 10 Ducat
1934—1298; 1935—600; 1936—633; 1937-192;
1938—20; 1951—100. 1 Ducat Kremnica—288;
2 Ducat Kremnica—159; 5 Ducat Kremnica—
70; 5 Ducat Wallenstein— ; 10 Ducat
Kremnica—68; 10 Ducat Wallenstein—

9. 5 Ducat 1934	....	$1800
10. 10 Ducat 1934	....	$3500

Issued to commemorate Wallenstein Coinage.
Obv: Bust of Wallenstein. Rev: Shield with
Crown.

DAHOMEY

1. 2500 Francs 1970	....	$10●
2. 5000 Francs 1970	....	$15●
3. 10,000 Francs 1970	....	$35●
4. 25,000 Francs 1970	....	$80●

Obv: 2500 Fr., Dance; 5000 Fr., Buffalos;
10,000 Fr., Hippopotamus; 25,000 Fr., 3 Co
joined Presidents Heads. All in proof. Con
sidered NCLT. There are 4 companion silve●
proof coins.

DOMINICAN REPUBLIC

1. 30 Peso 1955 . . . . **$250**

Issued to commemorate the 25th Anniversary of the rule of Trujillo. Obv: Head of Trujillo. Rev: Coat of Arms. The value of this coin has tended to follow the bullion market in spite of its low mintage, which in fact should make it a numismatic item. It has been "legal" for some time due to special decree of the US Treasury.

Rev.

2. 30 Peso 1973 . . . . **$135**

Issued to commemorate the 12th Central American Games. There is a companion 1 Peso Silver Piece of which 3000 issued in proof and 30,000 in unc. Obv: Coat of Arms. Rev: Emblem of Games and Legend.

Sizes and weights:
2500 Francs, 26 mm, 8.88 gms 900 fine
5000 Francs, 30 mm, 17.77 gms 900 fine
10,000 Francs, 40 mm, 35.55 gms 900 fine
25,000 Francs, 55 mm, 88.88 gms 900 fine

Mintages:
2000 numbered sets.

Sizes and weights:
30 Peso 1955, 32 mm, 29.6 gms 900 fine
30 Peso, 1973, 25 mm, 11.79 gms 900 fine

Mintages:
30 Peso 1955—32,750; 30 Peso 1973—25,000.

EGYPT

1. **20 Piastres 1938** $70
2. **50 Piastres 1938** $100
3. **100 Piastres 1938** $150
4. **500 Piastres 1938** $1200

Obv: Military Bust of King Farouk with Fez. Rev. Arabic Legend.

5. **1 Pound 1955 (yellow gold)** $105
6. **5 Pound 1955 (yellow gold)** $800

Issued to commemorate the Flight of Farouk in 1952 and Formation of the Republic. Obv: Chariot. Rev: Legend and Dates.

7. **1 Pound 1957 (red gold)** $115
8. **5 Pounds 1957 (red gold)** $850

(Same as 5 and 6 above)

9. **½ Pound 1958** $100

(Same as 5 and 6 above)

10. **1 Pound 1960** $110
11. **5 Pounds 1960** $475

Obv: Aswan Dam. Rev: Arabic Inscription

12. **5 Pounds 1964** $400
13. **10 Pounds 1964** $800

Obv: Diversion of the Nile. Rev. Arabic Inscription.

24

EGYPT (cont.)

14. 5 Pounds 1968 . . . . **$350**

Issued to commemorate the 1400th Anniversary of the Koran, the Arabic Bible. Obv: Koran on Globe. Rev: Inscription.

15. 1 Pound 1970 . . . . **$100**
16. 5 Pounds 1970 . . . . **$275**

Issued to honor Gamal Abdel Nasser. Obv: Bust of Nasser. Rev: Legend and Denomination.

17. 1 Pound 1973 . . . . **$100**
18. 5 Pounds 1973 . . . . **$275**

Issued to commemorate the 75th Anniversary of Egypt National Bank.

Sizes and weights:
20 Piastres, 15 mm, 1.7 gms 875 fine
50 Piastres, 18 mm, 4.2 gms 875 fine
100 Piastres, 22 mm, 8.5 gms 875 fine
500 Piastres, 35 mm, 42.5 gms 875 fine
1 Pound 1955,7,60, 24 mm, 8.5 gms 875 fine
5 Pounds 1955,7,60, 36 mm, 42.5 gms 875 fine

½ Pound, 20 mm, 4.25 gms 875 fine
5 Pounds 1964, 32 mm, 26 gms 875 fine
10 Pounds 1964, 40 mm, 52 gms 875 fine
5 Pounds 1968,70,73, 31 mm, 25.92 gms 875 fine
1 Pound 1970,73, 22 mm, 7.9 gms 875 fine

Mintages:*
20 Piastres–   ; 50 Piastres–   ; 100 Piastres
–   ; 500 Piastres–   ; 1 Pound
1955–16,096; 1 Pound 1957–10,000; 1 Pound
1960–5000; 1 Pound 1970–10,000; 1 Pound
1973–   ; 5 Pounds 1955–1000; 5 Pounds
1957–1000; 5 Pounds 1960–5000; 5 Pounds
1964–4000; 5 Pounds 1968–10,000; 5 Pound
1970–3000; 5 Pounds 1973–   ; 10 Pounds
1964–2000.

*Mintages unconfirmed

EQUATORIAL GUINEA

1. 250 Pesetas 1973 (A) **$55**
2. 250 Pesetas 1973 (B) **$55**
3. 500 Pesetas 1973 (A) **$85**
4. 500 Pesetas 1973 (B) **$85**
5. 500 Pesetas 1973 (C) **$85**
6. 500 Pesetas 1973 (D) **$85**
7. 750 Pesetas 1973 (A) **$100**
8. 750 Pesetas 1973 (B) **$100**
9. 750 Pesetas 1973 (C) **$100**
10. 750 Pesetas 1973 (D) **$100**
11. 1000 Pesetas 1973 . . . . **$150**
12. 5000 Pesetas 1973 . . . . **$650**

The 2–250 Pesetas have (A) Goya's Naked Maja and (B) Durer's "Praying Hands". The 4–500 Pesetas have (A) Pope John XXIII, (B) Abraham Lincoln, (C) Mahatma Ghandi and (D) Nicholi Lenin. The 4–750 Peseta coins issued to commemorate Rome as a capital city (A) has Obv: Roma Standing; (B) has Obv: Roma Seated: (C) has Obv: Forum and Coliseum; (D) has Obv: Winged head of Roma. Rev: on all is Tusks and Coat of Arms. The 1000 Peseta Obv: Jules Rimal Soccer Cup and scenes. The 5000 Peseta has President Macias. Rev: Crossed Tusks and Coat of Arms. These are all considered NCLT.

EQUATORIAL GUINEA (cont.)

Rev.

Sizes and weights:
250 Peseta, 18 mm, 3.52 gms 900 fine
500 Peseta, 23 mm, 7.05 gms 900 fine
750 Peseta, 30 mm, 10.57 gms 900 fine
1000 Peseta, 34 mm, 14.1 gms 900 fine
5000 Peseta, 60 mm, 70.52 gms 900 fine

Mintages:
3000 of each coin.

ETHIOPIA

1. 10 Dollars 1966 . . . . $60
2. 20 Dollars 1966 . . . . $120
3. 50 Dollars 1966 . . . . $200
4. 100 Dollars 1966 . . . . $450
5. 200 Dollars 1966 . . . . $900

Issued to commemorate the 75th Birthday of Emperor Haile Selassie. Obv: Bust of the Emperor. Rev: Coat of Arms. Issue is proof. Considered NCLT.

6. $50 Dollars (A) 1972 . . . . $250
7. $50 Dollars (B) 1972 . . . . $250
8. $50 Dollars (C) 1972 . . . . $250
9. $50 Dollars (D) 1972 . . . . $250
10. $100 Dollars 1972 . . . . $500

Issued to commemorate the 5 monarchs of modern Ethiopia. Rev: The Lion of Judah Symbol of the Nation. Obv: Busts of $50 (A) Theodros II; $50 (B) Yohannes IV; $50 (C) Menelik II; $50 (D) Empress Zewditu; $100 Haile Selassie. All proofs. Considered NCLT.

Note: Photos of this series could not be obtained. Photos are of 5 silver companion pieces which are same except for denomination.

Obv.

Sizes and weights:
10 Dollars, 18 mm, 4 gms 900 fine
20 Dollars, 24 mm, 8 gms 900 fine
50 Dollars, 33 mm, 20 gms 900 fine
100 Dollars, 45 mm, 40 gms 900 fine
200 Dollars, 53 mm, 80 gms 900 fine
50 Dollars 1972, 33 mm, 20 gms 900 fine
100 Dollars 1972, 45 mm, 40 gms 900 fine

Mintages:
The 1966 Series: 10 Dollars—27,998; 20 Dollars—25,281; 50 Dollars—14,977; 100 Dollars—11,330. The 1972 Series—10,000 sets.

27

FALKLAND ISLANDS

Announced: For 1975, a 3 piece set ½ pound, 1 pound, and 5 pound. Same size and weight as Great Britain issue of 1937.

FIJI ISLANDS

Announced: A $100 gold coin to be issued to commemorate the 100th Anniversary of Fiji's annexation by Great Britain an October 10, 1874. A $25 Silver companion crown will be issued. Obv: Bust of Queen Elizabeth II of Great Britain. Rev: Bust of Ratu Seru Cakobau a native chief in Fiji at time of annexation.

FRANCE

1. 100 Francs 1935,6 . . . . **$1000**

Obv: Winged Head of the Republic. Rev: Wheat, and Denomination. The Famous "Bazor" Coin, after its designer. A rare coin, especially the 1936. Also minted in 1929 and 1933.

Size and weight:
100 Francs, 20 mm, 6.5 gms 900 fine

Mintage:
1935—6,102,100; 1936—7,688,641. Virtually all melted under a decree of Sept. 26, 1936 by the Govt. of France, only a few thousand escaped, at most, for collectors, and usually only appear at auction.

FRENCH POLYNESIA

1. 10 Francs 1967 Piefort	**est. $500**
2. 20 Francs 1967 Piefort	**est. $600**
3. 50 Francs 1967 Piefort	**est. $800**

See Yeomans Current Coins of the World Y5, Y6, Y7 for description.
These are pattern pieces struck on double thickness planchets and are rarely offered for sale or auction.

Sizes and weights:
10 Francs, 22 mm, 11.7 gms 900 fine
20 Francs, 27 mm, 23.4 gms 900 fine
50 Francs, 33 mm, 58.5 gms 900 fine

Mintages:
20 of each.

FUJAIRAH

1. 25 Riyals 1968	**$85**
2. 50 Riyals 1968	**$125**
3. 100 Riyals 1968 (A)	**$200**
4. 100 Riyals 1968 (B)	**$200**
5. 100 Riyals 1968 (C)	**$200**
6. 100 Riyals 1968 (D)	**$200**
7. 100 Riyals 1970 (E)	**$200**
8. 100 Riyals 1970 (F)	**$200**
9. 200 Riyals 1968	**$350**

Rev: Coat of Arms. Obv: 25 Riyals, Bust of Richard Nixon; 50 Riyals Olympic Symbol, Torch; 100 Riyals (A) Apollo 12 Astronauts; 100 Riyals (B) Apollo 11 Astronauts; 100 Riyals (C), Apollo 13; 100 Riyals (D), Apollo 14; 100 Riyals (E), Pope Paul in Australia; 100 Riyals (F), Pope Paul in Phillipines; 200 Riyals, Bust of Alsharqi. All Proof. Considered NCLT.

FUJAIRAH (cont.)

Rev.

Sizes and weights:
25 Riyals, 21 mm, 5.18 gms 900 fine
50 Riyals, 28 mm, 10.36 gms 900 fine
100 Riyals, 35 mm, 20.73 gms 900 fine
200 Riyals, 50 mm, 41.46 gms 900 fine

Mintages:
25 Riyals—5000; 50 Riyals—5000; 100 Riyals—5000 of each; 200 Riyals—5000.

GABON

1. 10 Francs 1960 . . . . $80
2. 25 Francs 1960 . . . . $125
3. 50 Francs 1960 . . . . $175
4. 100 Francs 1960 . . . . $250

Dated 1960 but released in 1965 to commemorate Independence. Obv: Head of Leon Mba, President. Rev: Coat of Arms. All proof. Considered NCLT.

5. 1000 Francs 1969 . . . . $60
6. 3000 Francs 1969 . . . . $150
7. 5000 Francs 1969 . . . . $250
8. 10,000 Francs 1969 . . . . $500
9. 20,000 Francs 1969 . . . . $1000

Obv: Bust of President Bongo. Rev: 1000 Francs, Woodcutter; 3000 Francs, Coat of Arms; 5000 Francs, Tribal Mask; 10,000 Francs, Apollo 11 Landing on Moon; 20,000 Francs, Apollo 11 on Launching Pad.

Sizes and weights:
10 Francs, 19 mm, 3.2 gms 900 fine
25 Francs, 22.5 mm, 8 gms 900 fine
50 Francs, 26.5 mm, 16 gms 900 fine
100 Francs, 35 mm, 32 gms 900 fine
1000 Francs, 19 mm, 3.5 gms 900 fine
3000 Francs, 20.5 mm, 10.5 gms 900 fine
5000 Francs, 24 mm, 17.5 gms 900 fine
10,000 Francs, 30 mm, 35 gms 900 fine
20,000 Francs, 39 mm, 70 gms 900 fine

Mintages:
1960 series—500 sets plus 25,000 pieces of the 25 Francs; 1969 series—4000 sets.

GHANA

1. 2 Pounds 1960 . . . . **$175**

Obv: Bust of Nkruma. Rev: Crest and Date.

2. 2 Pounds 1965 . . . . **$200**

Issued to commemorate OAU Conference in Accra which never took place. Obv: Bust of Nkruma. Rev: Map of Africa, Legend "OAU Summit Conference 1965". Also issued in 38 mm–Rare.

3. 2 Pounds 1968 . . . . **$200**

Issued to commemorate the 1st Anniversary of the death of Lt. General Emmanuel Kwasi Kotoka. Obv: Bust of Kotoka. Rev: Coat of Arms, Date and Legend.

Size and weight:
2 Pounds, 28 mm, 15.99 gms 916²⁄₃ fine

Mintages:
2 Pounds 1960–15,200; 2 Pounds 1965–2020 2 Pounds 1968–2000. Also reported 38 mm var.–50.

GREAT BRITAIN

1. ½ Sovereign proof only **$35**
2. 1 Sovereign proof only **$37**
3. 2 Pounds proof only **$100**
4. 5 Pounds proof only **$150**

Issued to commemorate the coronation o King George VI. Obv: Bust of George. Rev: St George Slaying the Dragon.

5. ½ Sovereign specimen . . . . .Not issue
6. 1 Sovereign specimen . . . . .Not issue
7. 2 Pounds specimen . . . . .Not issue
8. 5 Pounds specimen . . . . .Not issue

Struck to commemorate the coronation o Queen Elizabeth II, and to continue the series None issued, all retained by the mint.

9. 1 Sovereign 1957–59, 62 on **$5**

Obv: Bust of Queen Elizabeth II. Rev: St George Slaying the Dragon.

GREAT BRITAIN (cont.)

Sizes and weights:
½ Sovereign, 18 mm, 3.99 gms 916²/₃ fine
Sovereign, 21 mm, 7.98 gms 916²/₃ fine
Pounds, 28 mm, 15.97 gms 916²/₃ fine
Pounds, 35 mm, 39.94 gms 916²/₃ fine

Mintages:
1937 Series—5501 of each; 1 Sovereign
1957-1968 Total—46,510,508.

Note: The one sovereign has become an internationally used bullion coin and its value tends to rise and fall with the value of gold bullion.

GREECE

1. **20 Drachma 1935** $2500
2. **100 Drachma 1935** $9000

Issued to commemorate the reestablishment of the Kingdom. Obv: Head of George II. Rev: Denomination in Wreath and a Crown.

3. **20 Drachma 1967** $300
4. **100 Drachma 1967** $700

Minted to commemorate the 1967 Revolution. Dated 1967. Issued in 1970. Obv: Soldier and Phoenix. Rev: Coat of Arms and denomination. There are 2 silver companion pieces.

Sizes and weights:
20 Drachma, 21 mm, 6.45 gms 900 fine
100 Drachma, 35 mm, 32.25 gms 900 fine

Mintages:
20 Drachma 1935—200; 20 Drachma 1967—10,000; 100 Drachma 1935—140; 100 Drachma 1967—20,000

Note: In 1960 an unofficial 20 Drachma gold coin was struck from the dies used for the 20 Drachma silver coin at the Royal Mint of England.

GUINEA

1. **1000 Francs 1969** $60
2. **2000 Francs 1969 (A)** $100
3. **2000 Francs 1969 (B)** $100
4. **2000 Francs 1969 (C)** $100
5. **5000 Francs 1969 (A)** $200
6. **5000 Francs 1969 (B)** $200
7. **10,000 Francs 1969** $400

Rev: Coat of Arms. Obv: 1000 Francs Heads of Robert and John Kennedy; 2000 Francs (A) Apollo 11 Land on Moon; 2000 Francs (B) Apollo 13; 2000 Francs (C) Soyez Spaceship; 5000 Francs Munich Scene and other Olympic Areas; 5000 Francs (B) Nasser; 10,000 Francs Bust of Ahmed Toure. All proofs. Considered NCLT.

Sizes and weights:
1000 Francs, 18 mm, 4 gms 900 fine
2000 Francs, 28 mm, 8 gms 900 fine
5000 Francs, 32 mm, 20 gms 900 fine
10,000 Francs, 45 mm, 40 gms 900 fine

Mintages:
1969 Series—4000 of each; 1970 Series—

Note: Guinea has produced a set of 7 5000 Francs Coin-Medals showing various Egyptian Princesses, Queens and Pharohs which are really not collectible numismatics, each with a weight of 20 gms and size of 32 mm 900 fine, valued at about $175 each.

HAITI

Series A:
1. 20 Gourdes 1968 . . . . $65
2. 50 Gourdes 1968 . . . . $100
3. 100 Gourdes 1968 . . . . $175
4. 200 Gourdes 1968 . . . . $300
5. 1000 Gourdes 1968 . . . . $1900

Rev: Coat of Arms. Obv: 20 Gourdes, Native with Machete; 50 Gourdes, Voodoo Dancer; 100 Gourdes, Girl with Machete; 200 Gourdes, Native Running with Machete; 1000 Gourdes, Bust of Duvalier. Considered NCLT. All proofs.

8. 2000 Francs 1970 (ND) (A) $100
9. 2000 Francs 1970 (ND) (B) $100
10. 5000 Francs 1970 (C) $200

Rev: Coat of Arms. Obv: (A) Apollo 12 in Flight; (B) Apollo 13 Insignia; (C) Bust of Nasser. All proofs. Considered NCLT.

Series B:
6. 30 Gourdes 1968 . . . . $65
7. 40 Gourdes 1968 . . . . $100
8. 60 Gourdes 1968 . . . . $120
9. 250 Gourdes 1968 . . . . $475
10. 500 Gourdes 1968 . . . . $900

Rev: Coat of Arms. Obv: 30 Gourdes, Citadelle; 40 Gourdes, Bust of Dessalines; 60 Gourdes, Bust of Petion; 250 Gourdes; Bust of Christophe; 500 Gourdes, Three Artists. All proofs.

HAITI (cont.)

11. **100 Gourdes 1973** $25
12. **200 Gourdes 1973** $50
13. **500 Gourdes 1973 (A)** $120
14. **500 Gourdes 1973 (B)** $120
15. **1000 Gourdes 1973** $240

In issue now. Price for the coins as above, for the proof set is 350£ ($875). Issued to commemorate the Inauguration of Jean Claude Duvalier, President for Life. Obv: Coat of Arms. Rev. 100G, Face of Christopher Colombus; 200 G, World Cup Soccer Symbol; 500 G(A), Haitian Girl on Beach; 500 G(B), Mother and Child; 1000 G, Bust of Jean Claude Duvalier. Considered NCLT.

Sizes and weights:
20 Gourdes, 18 mm, 3.96 gms 900 fine
30 Gourdes, 21 mm, 9.11 gms 585 fine
40 Gourdes, 26 mm, 12.15 gms 585 fine
50 Gourdes, 23 mm, 9.87 gms 900 fine
60 Gourdes, 32 mm, 18.22 gms 585 fine
100 Gourdes, 30 mm, 19.75 gms 900 fine
200 Gourdes, 40 mm, 39.49 gms 900 fine
250 Gourdes, 50 mm, 75.95 gms 585 fine
500 Gourdes, 70 mm, 151.9 gms 585 fine
1000 Gourdes, 60 mm, 197.48 gms 900 fine
100 Gourdes (1973), 15 mm, 1.45 gms 900 fine
200 Gourdes (1973), 18 mm, 2.91 gms 900 fine
500 Gourdes (1973), 25 mm, 7.28 gms 900 fine
1000 Gourdes (1973), 32 mm, 14.56 gms
   900 fine

Mintages:
1968 Series "A"—12,000 each; 1968 Series "B"—20,000 each; 1973 proofs—1250 sets; 1973 uncs—8000 sets.

Announced: A 1000 Gourdes coin to be issued in 1975 to commemorate the US Bicentennial, 32 mm, 13.1 gms 900 fine, Picturing the Battle of Savannah in which Haitian Troops fought with American colonists.

34

HUNGARY
(Peoples Republic of)

1. **50 Florins 1961** **$85**
2. **100 Florins 1961** **$130**
3. **500 Florins 1961** **$700**

Obv: Bust of Liszt. Rev: Lyre.

4. **50 Florins 1961** **$85**
5. **100 Florins 1961** **$130**
6. **500 Florins 1961** **$700**

Obv: Bust of Bartok. Rev: Lyre.

7. **100 Forint 1966** **$160**
8. **500 Forint 1966** **$600**
9. **1000 Forint 1966** **$850**

Issued to commemorate the 400th Anniversary of the War against the Turks. Obv: Bust of Nicholas Zrinyi. Rev: Battle Scene.

10. **500 Forint 1967** **$600**
11. **1000 Forint 1967** **$900**

Issued to commemorate 85th Birthday of Zoltan Kodaly. Obv: Bust of Kodaly. Rev: Peacock and Denomination.

HUNGARY (cont.)

12. **50 Forint 1968**	**$85**
13. **100 Forint 1968**	**$130**
14. **200 Forint 1968**	**$185**
15. **500 Forint 1968**	**$600**
16. **1000 Forint 1968**	**$900**

Issued to commemorate the 150th Birthday Anniversary of Dr. Ignaz Semmelweis. Obv: Bust of Semmelweis. Rev: Coat of Arms.

Sizes and weights:
(Note: "Florins" and "Forints" used interchangeably.)
50 Florin (1961), 18 mm, 3.86 gms 986 fine
100 Florin (1961), 22 mm, 7.67 gms 986 fine
500 Florin (1961), 40 mm, 38.38 gms 986 fine
50 Forint, 18 mm, 4.2 gms 900 fine
100 Forint, 22 mm, 8.41 gms 900 fine
200 Forint, 28 mm, 16.8 gms 900 fine
500 Forint, 40 mm, 42 gms 900 fine
1000 Forint, 46 mm, 84.1 gms 900 fine
1000 Forint (1968), 53 mm, 84.1 gms 900 fine

Mintages:
50 Florins 1961 (Liszt)–2500; 100 Florins 1961 (Liszt)–2500; 500 Florins 1961 (Liszt) –2500; 50 Florins 1961 (Bartok)–2500; 100 Florins 1961 (Bartok)–2500; 500 Florins 1961 (Bartok)–2500; 100 Forint 1966–3300; 500 Forint 1966–1100; 1000 Forint 1966–330; 500 Forint 1967–1000; 1000 Forint 1967–500; 50 Forint 1968–3500; 100 Forint 1968–3500; 200 Forint 1968–3500; 500 Forint 1968–3500; 1000 Forint 1968–7000.

The 1968 series mintage is unconfirmed.

Notes: a) In 1966 Hungary restruck the following coins in gold: 1929–100 Pengo; 1938 100 Pengo; 29 grams; 1938–100 Pengo, 43.5 grams;

and 1935, 40 Pengo. All coins in maximum mintages of 1000 pieces. The 1938–100 Pengo, 29 grams sold for $650 in June 1973 auction and $1400 at a April 1974 auction.
b) Also, the 100 Kronen of 1907 is being regularly restruck to put gold bullion on the market, there is no way to tell the original from the restrike, except the restrike is alway proof-like in appearance, and not usually circulated.

ICELAND

1. **500 Kroner 1961** **$400**

Obv: Head of Jon Sigurdsson. Rev: Coat of Arms and Denomination.

2. **10,000 Kroner 1974 – BU** **$300**
– Proof **$500**

Issued to commemorate the 1100th Anniversary of Settling of Iceland. Obv: Man in Boat holding Two Totems. Rev: 4 Legendary Icelandic Figures, Dates 874-1974.

Sizes and weights:
500 Kroner, 22 mm, 8.9 gms 900 fine
10,000 Kroner, 27.75 mm, 15.5 gms 900 fine

Mintages:
500 Kroner–10,000; 10,000 Kroner–proof–8000; 10,000 Kroner–BU–12,000.

ICELAND (cont.)

Note: The 500 Kroner has been heavily counterfeited. One telltale sign is a minor depression between the letters G & U, (near the top of the letters) in the name Sigurdsson on obv. Visable with the strong glass (or very good eyes).

INDIA

Bikanir State
1. 1 Mohur 1937 . . . . $190
2. ½ Mohur 1937 . . . . $145

Obv: Bust of Ruler. Rev: Indian Inscription.

Dhar State
3. 1 Mohur 1943 . . . . Unique

Obv: 2 Elephants Supporting Coat of Arms, Legend "Dhar State 1943". Rev: Inscription. Possibly unique. Owned by the author, and not cataloged anywhere. Authenticated by Numismatic Staff of Harmer Rooke, Numismatics Ltd. of N.Y. Believed to have been issued by Maharajah of Dhar from his private bullion stock during Japanese occupation of India, to pay for services.

Rajkot State
4. 1 Mohur 1945 Restrike $375

Obv: Rising Sun. Rev: Deer over Crescent between Tridents. Sold at June 1973 Auction for above value.

Sizes and weights:
½ Mohur (1937),   mm,   gms
1 Mohur (1937), 20 mm, 11.66 gms
1 Mohur (1943), 21 mm, 6.61 gms
1 Mohur (1945), 18 mm,   gms

Mintages:
Unknown

Note: The Indian government has been restriking, to order, early gold pieces of the British Rule with dates since 1841. They include the 1 Mohur of 1835, 1862, 1870, 1878, 1879; 5 Rupee of 1870, 1879; 10 Rupee 1870, 1879; 2 Mohur of 1835 and 15 Rupee of 1918.

INDONESIA

1. 25 Rupiah before 1952 . . . . $575

Obv: Head of Native. Rev: Coat of Arms on Body of Bird. A rare coin. Sold in Gilhausen II sale at $400. Offered Oct. 1974 at $575.

2. 2000 Rupiah 1970 . . . . $60
3. 5000 Rupiah 1970 . . . . $140
4. 10,000 Rupiah 1970 . . . . $250
5. 20,000 Rupiah 1970 . . . . $500
6. 25,000 Rupiah 1970 . . . . $600

INDONESIA (cont.)

Rev: Bird and Bank of Indonesia Monogram. Obv: 2000 Rupiah, Plumed Bird; 5000 Rupiah, Idol; 10,000 Rupiah, Balinese Dancer; 20,000 Rupiah, Deity; 25,000 Rupiah, Bust of Suharto. All proofs. Considered NCLT. Five companion silver proof pieces.

Rev.

Sizes and weights:
25 Rupiah, 28 mm, 14 gms 900 fine
2000 Rupiah, 18 mm, 4.93 gms 900 fine
5000 Rupiah, 30 mm, 12.34 gms 900 fine
10,000 Rupiah, 40 mm, 24.68 gms 900 fine
20,000 Rupiah, 50 mm, 49.37 gms 900 fine
25,000 Rupiah, 55 mm, 61.71 gms 900 fine

Mintage:
1970 series—4000 numbered sets, 25 Rupiah—rare.

Announced: 100,000 Rupiah 1974 part of Conservation coin series showing. Obv: Coat of Arms, Words "Bank of Indonesia". Rev: Komodo Dragon, 34 mm, 33.437 gms 900 fine 10,000 UNCS and 3000 proofs. Two companion silver pieces.

INDONESIA (cont.)

IRAN, see PERSIA

IRAQ

1. 5 Dinars 1971 . . . . proof $200
UNC $180

Issued to commemorate the Golden Jubilee of the Iraqi Army. Obv: Soldier in Helmet. Rev: Arabic Legend.

Size and weight:
5 Dinars, 28 mm, 13.6 gms 900 fine

Mintages:
proof—   ; unc—3000.

ISLE OF MAN

1. ½ Pound 1965 . . . . $1000 for
2. 1 Pound 1965 . . . . proof set
3. 5 Pounds 1965 . . . . $700 for
unc set

Issued to commemorate the 200th Anniversary of the purchase of Isle of Man by Great Britain. Rev: Arms in Shield. Obv: Bust of Queen Elizabeth II of Great Britain.

4. ½ Pound 1973 . . . . $45
5. 1 Pound 1973 . . . . $60
6. 2 Pounds 1973 . . . . $170
7. 5 Pounds 1973 . . . . $425

Obv: Bust of Queen Elizabeth II of Great Britain. Rev: St. George Slaying Dragon, and Date.

The proof set is offered in Great Britain at $1400.

39

ISLE OF MAN (cont.)

Sizes and weights:
½ Pound, 18 mm, 3.99 gms 916²⁄₃ fine
2 Pounds, 28 mm, 15.97 gms 916²⁄₃ fine
1 Pound, 21 mm, 7.98 gms 916²⁄₃ fine
5 Pounds, 35 mm, 39.94 gms 916²⁄₃ fine

Mintages:
½ Pound unc—15000 + 1500 in sets, proof—1000; 1 Pound unc—2000 + 1500 in sets; proof—1000; 5 Pounds unc—5000 + 1500 in sets, proof—1000; 1973 Series, 1250 sets.

ISRAEL

1. 20 Pounds 1960 . . . . $700

Issued to honor Dr. Theodore Herzl. Obv: Bust of Herzl. Rev: Menorah.

2. 50 Pounds 1962 . . . . $400
3. 100 Pounds 1962 . . . . $700

Issued to honor Dr. Chiam Weizmann, first president. Obv: Bust of Weizmann. Rev: Menorah.

4. 50 Pounds 1964 BU $1200
proof $6000

Issued to commemorate Bank of Israel Jubilee. Obv: Menorah. Rev: Double Cornucopia.

5. 100 Pounds 1967 . . . . $1300

Issued to honor Israel's Victory in the 1967 War (the Six-day War). Obv: Emblem of Israel Defense Force. Rev: The Western Wall of King Solomons Temple. A proof with some matt surfaces.

6. 100 Pounds 1968 . . . . $750

Issued to commemorate 20th Anniversary Independence. Obv: Temple of Solomon. Rev: Panoramic View of Jerusalem. Commonly called the Jerusalem Coin. Matt proof.

ISRAEL (cont.)

7. 100 Pounds 1969 .... $550

Issued in memory of fallen comrades. Obv: Monogram of Hebrew word "Sholom", meaning peace. Rev: Legend, Helmet and Branch. Proof coin with same matt surfaces.

8. 100 Pounds 1971 .... $800

Obv: Coat of Arms, Value and Date. Rev: Vertical Lines with Hebrew and English Legend, "Let My People Go". Proof coin.

9. 50 Pounds 1973 .... $200
10. 100 Pounds 1973 .... $300
11. 200 Pounds 1973 .... $800

Issued to commemorate 25th Anniversary of Independence. Obv: Menorah, Official Seal of State. Rev: Raised panel showing part of Declaration of Independence with signatures, legend.

12. 500 Pounds 1974 .... est. $700

Issued to commemorate David Ben Gurion. Obv: Bust of Ben Gurion. Rev: Menorah.

Sizes and weights:

20 Pounds 1960, 22 mm, 7.98 gms 916⅔ fine
50 Pounds 1962, 27 mm, 13.34 gms 916⅔ fine
100 Pounds 1962, 33 mm, 26.68 gms 916⅔ fine
50 Pounds 1964, 27 mm, 13.34 gms 916⅔ fine
100 Pounds 1967, 33 mm, 26.68 gms 916⅔ fine
100 Pounds 1968,69, 33 mm, 25.0 gms 800 fine
100 Pounds 1972, 30 mm, 22.0 gms 900 fine
50 Pounds 1973, 22 mm, 7.0 gms 900 fine
100 Pounds 1973, 27 mm, 13.5 gms 900 fine
200 Pounds 1973, 33 mm, 27.0 gms 900 fine
500 Pounds 1974, 35 mm, 28.0 gms 900 fine

Mintages:

Note: The figures shown are the net mintages in the hands of the public, after deducting coins which are held, as per report of the Bank of Israel in June 1974 by the Bank, and under Israeli Law will undoubtedly be melted. 20 Pounds 1960—10,075; 50 Pounds 1962—5941; 100 Pounds 1962—5940; 50 Pounds 1964—proof—841; 50 Pounds 1964—UNC—5201; 100 Pounds 1967—8020; 100 Pounds 1968—12,012; 100 Pounds 1969—12,009; 100 Pounds 1971—9,502; 50 Pounds 1973—30,752; 100 Pounds 1973—28,252; 200 Pounds 1973—18,251; 500 Pounds 1974—53,500 announced.

41

ISRAEL (cont.)

Note: Most of the 1973 series was issued in sets, as follows: 3 pc. set—18,249 sets; 2 pc. set—unknown. Most are retained as sets by collectors, resulting in very few single coins on the market.

ITALY

1. **100 Lire 1936** **$6000**
2. **100 Lire 1937 Reduced size** **$20,000**

Issued to commemorate the conquest of Ethiopia. Obv: Bust of Victor Emanuel, King of Italy. Rev: Standing Figure (Values on coins from Zurich Bank Auction of April 30, 1974).

3. **50 Lire 1936** .... .est. **$5000**

Obv: Head of Victor Emanuel, King of Italy. Rev: 2 Medallions, Capped with Eagle.

Sizes and weights:
100 Lire, 22.5 mm, 8.79 gms 900 fine
100 Lire (Reduced), 23 mm, 5.19 gms 900 fine
50 Lire, 19 mm, 4.39 gms 900 fine

Mintages:
100 Lire—812; 100 Lire (Reduced)—249; 50 Lire—790.

Note: Beware of counterfeits. These coins are rare.

IVORY COAST

1. **10 Francs 1966** **$675**
2. **25 Francs 1966** .... **for**
3. **50 Francs 1966** .... **the**
4. **100 Francs 1966** .... **set**

Obv: Bust of President Felix Houphouet Boigny. Rev: Elephant, Value, Legend. All proofs. Considered NCLT.

Sizes and weights:
10 Francs, 19 mm, 3.2 gms 900 fine
25 Francs, 22 mm, 8 gms 900 fine
50 Francs, 28 mm, 16 gms 900 fine
100 Francs, 34 mm, 32 gms 900 fine

Mintages:

JAMAICA

1. **20 Dollar 1972** .... proof **$100**
   BU **$70**

Issued to commemorate the 10th Anniversary of Independence. Obv: Coat of Arms, Denomination. Rev: Map of Jamaica, 3 Colombus Ships.

JAMAICA (cont.)

Size and weight:
20 Dollars, 27.1 mm, 14 gms 500 fine

Mintages:
Proof–3,000; UNC–12,000

Note: Probably NCLT. Jamaica claims that small numbers were placed on the market at face values. Contrary claims of reputable citizens who were on line at every bank before opening, in Kingston, the capitol, on day of issue and could not obtain coins.

Sizes and weights:
5 Pounds, 14.5 mm, 2.62 gms 916²⁄₃ fine
10 Pounds, 18 mm, 4.64 gms 916²⁄₃ fine
20 Pounds, 22.5 mm, 9.26 gms 916²⁄₃ fine
25 Pounds, 25 mm, 11.9 gms 916²⁄₃ fine
50 Pounds, 31 mm, 22.63 gms 916²⁄₃ fine

Mintages:
Uncirculated–8500 sets; proof–1500 sets.

JERSEY
(Bailiwick of)

1. 5 Pounds 1972 . . . .$600 for
2. 10 Pounds 1972 . . . . .the set
3. 20 Pounds 1972 . . . . .UNC
4. 25 Pounds 1972 . . . .$800 in
5. 50 Pounds 1972 . . . . .proof

Issued to commemorate the 25th Anniversary of the Marriage of Queen Elizabeth II of Great Britain to Prince Phillip. Obv: Bust of Queen Elizabeth II. Rév: 5 Pounds, A White Toothed Shrew; 10 Pounds Gold Torque; 20 Pounds Ormer Shell; 25 Pounds, Arms of Great Britain; 50 Pounds, Arms of Jersey.

JORDAN

1. 2 Dinars 1969 . . . .$70
2. 5 Dinars 1969 . . . .$150
3. 10 Dinars 1969 . . . .$300
4. 25 Dinars 1969 . . . .$750

Obv: Bust of King Hussein. Rev: 2 Dinars, Forum of Jepagh; 5 Dinars, Treasury Bldg; 10 Dinars, Bust of Pope Paul VI; 25 Dinars, Dome of the Rock. All proofs. Considered NCLT. Three companion silver proof pieces.

Obv.

Obv.

JORDAN (cont.)

Sizes and weights:
2 Dinars, 21 mm, 5.52 gms 900 fine
5 Dinars, 32 mm, 13.82 gms 900 fine
10 Dinars, 40 mm, 27.64 gms 900 fine
25 Dinars, 50 mm, 69.11 gms 900 fine

Mintages:
6000 numbered sets.

KATANGA

1. 5 Francs 1961 .... **$135**

Obv: Hand of Bananas. Rev: Baluba Cross, Date and Denomination. There are 2 companion pieces a 1 Franc and a 5 Franc in bronze.

Size and weight:
5 Francs, 26 mm, 13.33 gms 900 fine

Mintage:
20,000

KENYA

1. 100 Shilling 1966 ...... **$750 for set UNC**
2. 250 Shilling 1966 ...... **$1100 for set**
3. 500 Shilling 1966 ...... **proof**

Obv: Bust of President Jomo Kenyatta. Rev: 100 Shilling, Kenyatta's Fly Wisk; 250 Shilling, Cockerel; 500 Shilling, Mt. Kenya.

Obv.

44

KENYA (cont.)

Sizes and weights:
100 Shilling, 20 mm, 7.64 gms 916²⁄₃ fine
250 Shilling, 28 mm, 19.17 gms 916²⁄₃ fine
500 Shilling, 35 mm, 38.23 gms 916²⁄₃ fine

Mintages:
100 Shilling—7500; 250 Shilling—1000; 500 Shilling—500.
Issued as 500—3 piece sets, the balance of the 250 and 100 Shilling coins being sold individually. Information regarding how many are proof and how many uncirculated is not available.

KUWAIT

1. 5 Dinars 1961. . . . . **est. $475**

Obv: Denomination in Circle. Rev: Dhow Sailing. A rare coin. Has not been offered in past 3 years to author's knowledge.

Size and weight:
5 Dinar, 28 mm,   gms 916²⁄₃ fine

Mintage:
1000

LAOS

1. 4000 Kip 1971	. . . .	$70
2. 8000 Kip 1971	. . . .	$100
3. 20,000 Kip 1971	. . . .	$250
4. 40,000 Kip 1971	. . . .	$500
5. 80,000 Kip 1971	. . . .	$1000

Issued to commemorate coronation of King. Obv: Bust of King Sri Savang Vatthana. Rev: Three Headed Elephant. Considered NCLT.

LAOS (cont.)

Sizes and weights:
4000 Kip, 17 mm, 4 gms 900 fine
8000 Kip, 22 mm, 8 gms 900 fine
20,000 Kip, 28 mm, 20 gms 900 fine
40,000 Kip, 36.5 mm, 40 gms 900 fine
80,000 Kip, 48 mm, 80 gms 900 fine

Mintage:
10,000 numbered sets

LESOTHO

Series (A):
1. 1 Maloti 1966 . . . . $100
2. 2 Maloti 1966 . . . . $125
3. 4 Maloti 1966 . . . . $300

Obv: Bust of King Moshoeshoe clothed. Rev: Coat of Arms. All proofs. Considered NCLT.

Series (B):
4. 2 Maloti 1966 . . . . Rare
5. 4 Maloti 1966 . . . . Rare

6. 10 Maloti 1966 . . . . Rare
7. 20 Maloti 1966 . . . . Rare

Obv: Bust of King Moshoeshoe. Rev: Coat of Arms. Reported pattern pieces. All proofs. Less than 10 sets.

8. 1 Maloti 1969 . . . . $70
9. 2 Maloti 1969 . . . . $100
10. 4 Maloti 1969 . . . . $175
11. 10 Maloti 1969 . . . . $300
12. 20 Maloti 1969 . . . . $600

Issued to commemorate F.A.O. of U.N. Obv: Bust of King Moshoeshoe clothed. Rev: 1 Maloti, Rider on Horseback; 2 Maloti, Farmer; 4 Maloti, Ram; 10 Maloti, Man Leading Water Buffalo; 20 Maloti, 2 Sheep. All proofs. Considered NCLT.

LESOTHO (cont.)

Sizes and weights:
1 Maloti, 20 mm, 4 gms 916²/₃ fine
2 Maloti, 22 mm, 8 gms 916²/₃ fine
4 Maloti, 28 mm, 16 gms 916²/₃ fine
10 Maloti, 40 mm, 40 gms 916²/₃ fine
20 Maloti, 50 mm, 80 gms 916²/₃ fine

Mintages:
1966 Series A–500 of each; 1966 Series B–10 of each, 1969 Series–3000 of each.

LIBERIA

1. 20 Dollars 1964 (Red Gold) . . **proof $150**
UNC $125
2. 20 Dollars 1964 (Yellow Gold) **$150**

Obv: Head of William Tubman. Rev: Coat of Arms. Proof has "L" above date.

3. 25 Dollars 1965 . . . . **proof $150**
BU $125

Obv: Head of William Tubman. Rev: Providence Island, place of first landing of slaves from USA in 1822. Proof has "L" above date.

4. 12 Dollars 1965 . . . . **Rare**
5. 30 Dollars 1965 . . . . **Rare**

Reputedly patterns. Both proof condition. Obv: Bust of William Tubman. Rev: Coat of Arms.

6. 25 Dollars 1970 . . . . **$125**

Issued to commemorate the 75th Birthday of President Tubman. Obv: Bust of Tubman, Legend "Diamond Jubilee, 1895-1970". Rev: House of Tubman's Birth, Harper, Maryland County, Liberia.

7. 2½ Dollars 1974 . . . . **$835**
8. 5 Dollars 1974 . . . . **for**
9. 10 Dollars 1974 . . . . **the**
10. 20 Dollars 1974 . . . . **set**

Obv: 2½ Dollars, The Capitol; 5 Dollars, Sailing Ship; 10 Dollars, Women's Head; 20 Dollars, Head of president Tolbert. Rev: Coat of Arms, Denomination.

LIBERIA (cont.)

Sizes and weights:
20 Dollars, 27 mm, 18.65 gms 900 fine
25 Dollars, 30 mm, 23.3 gms 900 fine
12 Dollars, 21 mm, 6.0 gms 900 fine
30 Dollars, 30 mm, 15 gms 900 fine
2½ Dollars, 17 mm, 4.18 gms 900 fine
5 Dollars, 21 mm, 8.35 gms 900 fine
10 Dollars, 27 mm, 16.72 gms 900 fine
20 Dollars (1974), 34 mm, 33.43 gms 900 fine

Mintages:
$20 1964—10,200 (Includes 200 proofs); $25
1965—3100 (Includes 100 proofs); $12
1965—Nominal number of patterns; $30
1965—Nominal number of patterns; $25
1970—   ;
1974 Series—250 sets.

LIECHTENSTEIN

1. 10 Franken 1946	**$175**
2. 20 Franken 1946	**$300**

Obv: Head of Franz Joseph II. Rev: Coat of Arms.

3. 25 Franken 1956	**$150**
4. 50 Franken 1956	**$225**
5. 100 Franken 1952	**$2200**

Obv: Head of Prince Franz Joseph II and Princess Gina. Rev: Coat of Arms.

LIECHTENSTEIN (cont.)

6. 25 Franken 1961 . . . . *
7. 50 Franken 1961 . . . . *

Obv: Bust of Franz Joseph II, Prince. Rev: Coat of Arms, denomination.

*Not Issued.

8. 1 Ducat 1728 Restrike $80
9. 1 Ducat 1758 Restrike $80
10. 1 Ducat 1778 Restrike $80
11. 10 Ducat 1616 Restrike . . . . . . est. $300
12. 10 Ducat 1728 Restrike . . . . . . est. $300
13. 1 Gulden Taler Klippe 1619 . . . . . . $300
14. Vereinstaler 1862 Restrike . . . . est. $300

Rev: Coat of Arms. Obv: 1728 Ducat, Bust of Joseph John Adam; 1758 Ducat, Bust of Joseph Wenzel; 1778 Ducat, Bust of Franz Joseph I; 1616 10 Ducat, Prince Charles; 1718 10 Ducat, Joseph John Adam. 1 Gulden Taler Klippe, diamond shaped coin bust of Carl 1st. Vereinstaler 1862, Bust of Johann II. Considered NCLT.

Note: The symbol "M" appears on all restrikes of Liechtenstein.

LIECHTENSTEIN (cont.)

Sizes and weights:
10 Franken, 18 mm, 3.22 gms 900 fine
20 Franken, 22 mm, 6.45 gms 900 fine
25 Franken, 18 mm, 5.64 gms 900 fine
50 Franken, 26 mm, 11.29 gms 900 fine
100 Franken, 35 mm, 32.25 gms 900 fine
1 Ducat Restrike, 20 mm, 3.5 gms 986 fine
10 Ducat Restrike, 44 mm, 35 gms 986 fine
1 Gulden Taler Klippe, 23 mm, 10 gms 986 fine
1 Vereinstaler, 32 mm, 29.5 gms 900 fine

Mintages:
10 Franken—10,000; 20 Franken—10,000; 25 Franken—15,000; 50 Franken—15,000; 100 Franken—4000; 25 Franken 1961—20,000*; 50 Franken 1961—20,000*.

*Not issued.

Restrikes—Mintages: (Maximum)
10 Ducat 1616—50,000; 1 Gulden Taler—Klippe 1619—100,000; 10 Ducat 1728—50,000; 1 Ducat 1728—100,000; 1 Ducat 1758—100,000; 1 Ducat 1778—100,000; 1 Vereinstaler 1862—50,000.

LUNDY ISLAND

1. Half Puffin . . . . Rare
2. One Puffin . . . . Rare

Obv: Head. Rev: Puffin Bird.

Sizes and weights:
Half Puffin, 21 mm,   gms 900 fine
Puffin, 28 mm,   gms 900 fine

Mintages:
25 of each—presentation pieces.

LUXEMBOURG

1. 20 Francs 1953 . . . . $80

Issued to commemorate Marriage of Prince Jean and Princess Josephine Charlotte of Belgium. Obv: Cojoined Heads of Prince and Princess. Rev: Coat of Arms. Sometimes disputed as a coin since no denomination appears. Considered a numismatic collectible.

5. 100 Francs Essai . . . . Rare

Obv: Head of Prince Jean. Rev: John the Blind on Horseback.

2. 20 Francs 1953 (Jean) $70
3. 20 Francs 1953 (Charlotte) $70

Obv: of Each Coin One Head. Rev: Geometric Pattern. Sometimes disputed as a coin since no denomination appears. Considered a numismatic collectible.

6. 5 Francs 1962 Essai $1000

Obv: Head of Charlotte. Rev: Design.

4. 40 Francs 1963 . . . . $100

Obv: Contessa Ermesinde standing figure with her name. Rev: Shield and Legend and Date 1196-1247.

7. 250 Francs 1963 Essai $1300

Issued to honor the Millenium of the Duchy of Luxembourg. Companion Silver piece available in $75 range. Only known sale of 250 Franc Swiss Auction, April 30, 1974.

8. 100 Francs 1964 Essai $900
9. 1 Franc 1965 Essai $500
10. 10 Francs 1971 Essai $700
11. 5 Francs 1971 Essai $550

Obv: On all above, Bust of Jean Grand Duke of Luxembourg. Rev: 100 Fr. 1964, Coat of Arms; 1 Fr. 1965 and 5 Fr. 1971, Wreath, Denomination and Crown; 10 Fr. 1971, Date, Denomination and Crown.

Sizes and weights:
20 Francs, 20 mm, 6.45 gms 900 fine
40 Francs, 27 mm, 12.9 gms 900 fine
100 Francs, 37 mm, 32.25 gms 900 fine
100 Francs 1964, 34 mm,   gms 900 fine
1 Franc 1965, 20 mm,   900 fine
10 Francs 1971, 27 mm,   gms 900 fine
5 Francs 1971, 25 mm,   gms 900 fine
250 Francs 1963, 42 mm,   gms 900 fine

Mintages:
20 Francs (2 heads)—25,200; 20 Francs (Jean)—   ; 20 Francs (Charlotte)--   ; 40 Francs—1963   ; 100 Francs (John the Blind)—unknown; 250 Francs 1963—200; 5 Francs 1962—50; 100 Francs 1964—200; 1 Francs 1965—250; 10 Francs 1971—250; 5 Francs 1971—250.

MALAYSIA

1. 100 Ringgit 1971 . . . . $150

Obv: Bust of Tunku Abdul Rahman Putra. Rev: Building, 14 Point Star and Denomination.

Size and weight:
100 Ringgit, 26 mm, 18.59 gms 900 fine

Mintage :
100,000

MALI

1. 10 Francs 1967 . . . . $675
2. 25 Francs 1967 . . . . for
3. 50 Francs 1967 . . . . the
4. 100 Francs 1967 . . . . set

Obv: Head of Pres. Modibo Keita. Considered NCLT.

Sizes and weights:
10 Francs, 18 mm, 3.2 gms 900 fine
25 Francs, 23 mm, 8 gms 900 fine
50 Francs, 28 mm, 16 gms 900 fine
100 Francs, 34 mm, 32 gms 900 fine

Mintage:
10,000 sets

MALTA

1. 5 Pounds 1972 . . . . $500
2. 10 Pounds 1972 . . . . for
3. 20 Pounds 1972 . . . . the
4. 50 Pounds 1972 . . . . set

Obv: 5 Pounds, Map of Malta and Torch; 10 Pounds, Isometric Design; 20 Pounds, Bird, Sea and Rising Sun; 50 Pounds, Statue of Neptune. Rev: Coat of Arms. Two silver companion pieces exist in 1 & 2 Pounds.

MALTA (cont.)

Rev.

5. 10 Pounds 1973 . . . . **$425**
6. 20 Pounds 1973 . . . . **for**
7. 50 Pounds 1973 . . . . **the set**

Obv: 10 Pounds, City Scene; 20 Pounds, Arch and Statue; 50 Pounds, Building. Rev: Coat of Arms. Two silver companion pieces in 1 & 2 Pounds.

8. 10 Pounds 1974 . . . . **$325**
9. 20 Pounds 1974 . . . . **for**
10. 50 Pounds 1974 . . . . **the set**

Obv: 10 Pounds, National Flower of Malta; 20 Pounds, Gozo Boat with Lateen Sails; 50 Pounds, Likeness of First Maltese Coin. Rev: Coat of Arms. Two silver companion pieces in 2 & 4 Pounds.

Sizes and weights:
5 Pounds 1972, 18 mm, 2.98 gms 900 fine
10 Pounds 1972, 21 mm, 5.96 gms 900 fine
20 Pounds 1972, 26 mm, 12 gms 900 fine
50 Pounds 1972, 34 mm, 30.2 gms 900 fine
10 Pounds 1973,4, 18 mm, 2.98 gms 916$\frac{2}{3}$ fine
20 Pounds 1973,4, 21 mm, 5.96 gms 916$\frac{2}{3}$ fine
50 Pounds 1973,4, 27 mm, 14.9 gms 916$\frac{2}{3}$ fine

Mintages:
1972 Series—8000 sets; 1973 Series—10,000 sets; 1974 Series—

Note: The Knights of Malta (Sovereign Military Order of Malta), a private religious order issues coins to raise revenue, with the approval of the Government of Malta. They are coin/medals and not generally considered as numismatic collectibles. Mintages under 1000 on the gold pieces. Denomination used is the Scudi.

MAURITIUS

1. 200 Rupee 1971 . . . . **proof $600**
UNC $275

Obv: Bust of Queen Elizabeth II of Great Britain. Rev: Scene of Two Legendary Lovers, Paul and Eugiene Sitting.

Size and weight:
27.76 mm, 15.56 gms 900 fine

Mintages:
Proof—750; UNC—2500.

Announced: 1000 Rupees 1975 part of Conservation coin series. Obv: Bust of Queen Elizabeth II of Great Britain. Rev. Mauritius Flycatcher 34 mm, 33.4 gms 900 fine. 10,000 in UNC and 3000 proofs.

MEXICO

Mexican Gold Coins issued since 1934 have been and are basically traded as gold bullion. The Mexican mint produces "Restrikes", as a business. Some collectors do retain either type pieces or date sets. Values go up & down with the price of bullion daily.

1. 2 Peso 1944-48 . . . . **$10**
2. 2½ Peso 1944-48 . . . . **$13**
3. 5 Peso 1955 . . . . **$25**
4. 10 Peso 1959 . . . . **$50**
5. 20 Peso 1959 . . . . **$100**
6. 50 Peso 1943 . . . . **$230**
7. 50 Peso 1944-47 . . . . **$220**

Obv: 2 Peso, Eagle; 2½ Peso, 5 Peso and 10 Peso, Head of Hidalgo; 20 Peso, Aztec Calendar; 50 Peso, Winged Victory (in 1943 no denomination) other dates have denomination and purity of gold. Rev: 2 Peso, Denomination. All other values show the Mexican Eagle.

Sizes and weights:
2 Peso, 13 mm, 1.66 gms 900 fine
2½ Peso, 15.5 mm, 2.08 gms, 900 fine
5 Peso, 19 mm, 4.16 gms 900 fine
10 Peso, 22.5 mm, 8.33 gms 900 fine
20 Peso, 27.5 mm, 16.66 gms 900 fine
50 Peso, 37 mm, 41.66 gms 900 fine

Mintages:
2 Peso 1944–10,000; 1945–865,000;
1946–167,500; 1947–25,000; 1948–45,000.
2½ Peso 1944–20,000; 1945–1,100,000;
1946–163,000; 1947–24,000; 1948–63,000.
5 Peso 1955–354,000. 10 Peso 1959–50,000.
20 Peso 1959–12,500. 50 Peso 1944–592,900;
1945–1,012,299; 1946–1,587,600; 1947–
Restruck regularly.

Note: The Mexico 50 Peso is being counterfeited in .720 fine gold, with the genuine coin being in .900 fine gold, Purchase from responsible dealers only is recommended.

MEXICO

Commemorative Gold

The Mexican Mint has produced numerous pieces of commemorative gold in limited editions, listed below. Mintages are reported, but are unverified. Sizes and weights are identical to regular Mexican gold issues listed above.

1. 10 Peso 1953 . . . . $80
2. 20 Peso 1953 . . . . $125

Issued to commemorate 200th Anniversary of the Birth of Hidalgo. Obv: Bust of Hidalgo and Church in background. Rev: Mexican Eagle.

3. 10 Peso 1957 . . . . $80
4. 50 Peso 1957 . . . . $300

Issued to commemorate the 100th Anniversary of the Mexican Constitution. Obv: 10 Peso, Bust of Juarez. Rev: Mexican Eagle. Obv: 50 Peso, Statue and Legend. Rev: Scene of Constitutional Convention.

5. 20 Peso 1957 . . . . **$125**

Issued to commemorate Carranza. Obv: Face of Carranza. Rev: Church.

8. 50 Peso Zapata **$300**

Issued to commemorate Zapata. Obv: Zapata on Horse, with Farmer Standing. Rev: Sun Shining Over Mexican Flag.

6. 20 Peso 1962 . . . . **$125**
7. 50 Peso 1962 . . . . **$300**

Issued to commemorate the 5th of May, 1862 Battle of Puebla. Obv: 20 Peso, Bust and Legend; 50 Peso, Man on Horse; Rev: Mexican Eagle.

9. 50 Peso Guanajuato **$275**

Obv: Church with Don Quixote and Sancho Panza on steps. Rev: Crest and Legend;

Note: Many other minor issues were minted in editions of 100 or less for presentation purposes.

57

MONACO

Prior to 1904 Monaco issued circulating gold coins. From 1943 on, Essai, and presentation pieces were minted, many from dies used for smaller denominations. These coins are rarely available, and many of the values shown are taken from an auction at the Zurich Bank on April 30, 1974, at which a good number of the pieces were sold.

1. 500 Francs 1934 . . . . Rare
2. 1 Franc (ND) 1943* . . . . $
3. 1 Franc (ND) 1943** . . . . $
4. 2 Francs (ND) 1943* . . . . $
5. 2 Francs (ND) 1943** . . . . $
6. 5 Francs 1945* $400
7. 5 Francs 1945** $1100
8. 10 Francs 1946* $350
9. 10 Francs 1946** . . . . est. $500
10. 20 Francs 1947* $450
11. 20 Francs 1947** . . . . est. $700

Obv: Head of Louis II. Rev. Coat of Arms and denomination.

*Normal Thickness
**Double Thickness

12. 10 Francs 1950* $600
13. 10 Francs 1950** $700
14. 20 Francs 1950* $900
15. 20 Francs 1950** $1000
16. 50 Francs 1950* . . . . est. $800
17. 50 Francs 1950** $950
18. 100 Francs 1950* . . . . est $800
19. 100 Francs 1950** $950
20. 100 Francs 1956* $600
21. 100 Francs 1956** . . . . est. $750

Obv: Head of Rainier III. Rev: Coat of Arms.

22. 5 Francs 1960* . . . . est $400
23. 5 Francs 1960** . . . . est. $600
24. 1 Franc 1960* . . . . est. $250
25. 1 Franc 1960** . . . . est. $350
26. 50 Centimes 1962* . . . . est. $300
27. 50 Centimes 1962** . . . . est. $550
28. 20 Centimes 1962* . . . . est. $200
29. 20 Centimes 1962** . . . . est. $350
30. 10 Centimes 1962* . . . . est. $200
31. 10 Centimes 1962** . . . . est. $350
32. ½ Franc 1965 . . . . est. $300
33. 5 Francs 1965 . . . . est. $450

Obv: Bust of Rainier III, Prince of Monaco. Rev: Coat of Arms and on the Centimes, Coat of Arms and Standing Figure.

MONACO (cont.)

34. 10 Francs 1965 . . . . est. $650

Obv: Bust of Charles III. Rev. Coat of Arms and date.

35. 200 Francs 1966 . . . . proof $650
BU $450

Issued to commemorate the 10th Anniversary of the marriage of Prince Rainier to Princess Grace. Obv: Cojoined Heads of Prince Rainier and Princess Grace. Rev: Coat of Arms, Denomination and Legend.

Sizes and weights:
500 Francs 1934,   mm, 31.19 gms 900 fine
1 Franc 1943, 22 mm, 8 gms 900 fine
1 Franc 1943, 22 mm, 16 gms 900 fine
2 Francs 1943, 26 mm, 16 gms 900 fine
2 Francs 1943, 26 mm, 32 gms 900 fine
5 Francs 1945, 30 mm,   gms 900 fine
5 Francs 1945, 30 mm,   gms 900 fine
10 Francs 1946, 26 mm,   gms 900 fine
10 Francs 1946, 26 mm,   gms 900 fine
20 Francs 1947, 30 mm,   gms 900 fine
20 Francs 1947, 30 mm,   gms 900 fine
10 Francs 1950, 20 mm, 10.5 gms 900 fine
10 Francs 1950, 20 mm, 21 gms 900 fine

20 Francs 1950, 23 mm, 14.5 gms 900 fine
20 Francs 1950, 23 mm, 29 gms 900 fine
50 Francs 1950, 26 mm, 20.5 gms 900 fine
50 Francs 1950, 26 mm, 41 gms 900 fine
100 Francs 1950, 30 mm, 25.5 gms 900 fine
100 Francs 1950, 30 mm, 51 gms 900 fine
100 Francs 1956, 23 mm, 12 gms 900 fine
100 Francs 1956, 23 mm, 24 gms 900 fine
5 Francs 1960, 28 mm, 20.5 gms 920 fine
5 Francs 1960, 28 mm, 41 gms 920 fine
1 Franc 1960, 23 mm, 11.75 gms 920 fine
1 Franc 1960, 23 mm, 23.5 gms 920 fine
50 Centimes 1962, 26 mm, 16.5 gms 920 fine
50 Centimes 1962, 26 mm, 33 gms 920 fine
20 Centimes 1962, 24 mm, 8.75 gms 920 fine
20 Centimes 1962, 24 mm, 17.5 gms 920 fine
10 Centimes 1962, 20 mm, 6.5 gms 920 fine
10 Centimes 1962, 20 mm, 13 gms 920 fine
½ Franc 1965, 19 mm, 9.25 gms 920 fine
5 Francs 1965,   mm, 20.5 gms 920 fine
10 Francs 1965, 36 mm, 42.5 gms 920 fine
200 Francs 1966, 36 mm, 32 gms 920 fine

Mintages:
100 Francs 1950 Normal—500; 100 Francs 1950 Double—350; 50 Francs 1950 Normal—500; 50 Francs 1950 Double—350; 20 Francs 1950 Normal—500; 20 Francs 1950 Double—350; 10 Francs 1950 Normal—500; 10 Francs 1950 Double—350; 100 Francs 1956 Normal—500; 100 Francs 1956 Double—20; 5 Francs 1960 Normal—500; 5 Francs 1960 Double—25; 1 Franc 1960 Normal—500; 1 Franc 1960 Double—25; 50 Centimes 1962 Normal—500; 50 Centimes 1962 Double—25; 20 Centimes 1962 Normal—500; 20 Centimes 1962 Double—25; 10 Centimes 1962 Normal—500; 10 Centimes 1962 Double—25; ½ Franc 1965—1000; 5 Francs 1966—500; 10 Francs 1966—1000; 200 Francs 1967—5000 unc and 1000 proofs.

MOROCCO

1. 500 Francs 1953 . . . . **$300**

Obv: Bust of Mulai Mohamed Ben Youssef. Rev: Umbrella, Crown, Star. A rare presentation piece. Last appeared in Quality Sales Auction of Sept. 11, 1973. Sold at above price.

Size and weight:
500 Francs, 25 mm,   gms 900 fine

Mintage:
250

MUSCAT AND OMAN

1. 15 Ryals 1962 (1391 AH) **$175**

Obv: Crossed Daggers in Circle. Rev: Denomination.

2. 25 Baiza 1970 . . . . **$300**
3. 50 Baiza 1970 . . . . **for the**
4. 100 Baiza 1970 . . . . **set**
5. 1 Ryal 1959 . . . . **$**
6. ½ Rial 1970 . . . . **est. $250**
7. 1 Rial 1970 . . . . **$400**

These are gold strikes of lower denomination coins and were made in limited issue as presentation pieces. The prices above from Sept. 1973 Auction.

Sizes and weights:
15 Ryals 1962, 20 mm, 7.98 gms 916²⁄₃ fine
25 Baiza,   mm, 5.58 gms 916²⁄₃ fine
50 Baiza,   mm, 12.44 gms 916²⁄₃ fine
100 Baiza,   mm, 24.9 gms 916²⁄₃ fine
1 Ryal 1959, 36 mm,   gms 916²⁄₃ fine

Mintages:
1 Ryal 1959–100; ½ Ryal 1962–100; 15 Ryal 1962–   ; 1 Ryal 1970–250; ½ Ryal 1970–50; 25, 50, 100 Baiza–250 each.

NEPAL

1. ½ Mohar 1934-38 . . . . **$100**
2. 1 Mohar 1934-38 . . . . **$175**
3. 2 Mohar 1934-38 . . . . **$225**

Continuation of a Series from 1912. Obv: Inscription in Circle Surrounded by Inscription in Square. Rev: Pattern with Inscriptions.

NEPAL (cont.)

4. ¼ Rupee 1938 . . . . $85
5. ½ Rupee 1938-48 . . . . $100
6. 1 Rupee 1938-48 . . . . $175
7. 2 Rupee 1948 . . . . $225

Design similiar to #1-3 above.

8. ⅛ Rupee 1953 . . . . $65
9. ¼ Rupee 1953 . . . . $85
10. ½ Rupee 1953 . . . . $120
11. 1 Rupee 1953 . . . . $185

Obv: Head of Tribhubana. Rev: Mountain and Sun in Wreath.

12. ⅕ Rupee 1955 . . . . $65
13. ¼ Rupee 1955 . . . . $85
14. ½ Rupee 1955,62 . . . . $120
15. 1 Rupee 1955,62 . . . . $185
16. 2 Rupee 1955 . . . . $235

Obv: Circle Surrounded by Square Surrounded by Circle. Rev: Panelled Legend with Circle.

17. ⅕ Rupee 1956 . . . . $65
18. ½ Rupee 1956 . . . . $120
19. 1 Rupee 1956 . . . . $185

Issued to commemorate the coronation of Mahendra as King. Obv: Plummed Crown. Rev: Legend and Sword within Wreath.

Sizes and weights:
½ Mohar 20, mm, 2.88 gms 916⅔ fine
1 Mohar, 26 mm, 5.76 gms 916⅔ fine
2 Mohar, 26 mm, 11.52 gms 916⅔ fine
⅛ Rupee,   mm,   gms 900 fine
⅕ Rupee,   mm, 0.70 gms 900 fine
¼ Rupee,   mm, 1.44 gms 900 fine
½ Rupee,   mm, 2.88 gms 900 fine
1 Rupee,   mm, 5.76 gms 900 fine
2 Rupee,   mm, 11.52 gms 900 fine

Mintages:

Announced: One Asarafi, part of Conservation Coin Series. Obv: Bust of King Birendra Bir Bikram Shah Deve. Rev: The Great Indian Rhino, 34 mm 33.4 gms, .900 fine. Issue of 10,000 uncs and 3000 proofs. Two companion silver pieces.

NETHERLANDS

1. 1 Ducat 1937, and 1960 . . . . $400

Obv: Standing Man. Rev: 4 Line Legend. Part of a continuing series over 200 years old. Value shown above is for a proof of the 1960 piece, Zurich Bank Auction of April 30, 1974.

(Same photo Netherlands East Indies)

NETHERLANDS (cont.)

Size and weight:
1 Ducat, 20 mm, 3.49 gms 986 fine

Mintages:
1937–116,600; 1960–3,605.

Note: See Netherlands East Indies for similiar issues

NETHERLANDS EAST INDIES

1. 1 Ducat 1934 . . . .$28

Obv: Knight Standing. Rev: Square, enclosing a legend.

Note: These coins are produced as trade coins, and today are considered bullion coins. Its value rises and falls daily with the value of gold. Early issues in the continuing series which goes back to the 16th century are of course, numismatic items, with increased value, beyond that noted above.

Size and weight:
1 Ducat, 20 mm, 3.49 gms 986 fine

Mintages:

NEW HEBRIDES

1. 10 Francs 1967 Piefort . . . . est. **$500**
2. 20 Francs 1967 Piefort . . . . est. **$600**
3. 50 Francs 1967 Piefort . . . . est. **$800**

See Yeomans "Current Coins of the World", for description Y1, Y2, Y3. These are pattern pieces struck on double thickness planchets, and are rarely offered for sale, or auction.

Sizes and weights:
10 Francs, 22 mm, 11.7 gms 900 fine
20 Francs, 27 mm, 23.4 gms 900 fine
50 Francs, 33 mm, 58.5 gms 900 fine

Mintage:
20 of each.

NICARAGUA

1. 50 Cordobas 1967 . . . . **$475**

Issued to commemorate the 100th Birthday of the poet Ruben Dario. Obv: Bust of Ruben Dario. Rev: Coat of Arms surrounded by Triangle. Generally a scarce coin. Rumor has it that a good number of the original mintage was destroyed in an earthquake in Managua, Nicaragua.

NICARAGUA (cont.)

Size and weight:
50 Cordobas, 35 mm, 32 gms 900 fine

Mintage:
16,000

Announced: Two gold coins for 1975, in 900 fine, being 1000 and 2000 Cordobas. Also three silver companion pieces being produced by the Royal Mint, London, for the Central Bank of Nicaragua, to commemorate US Bicentennial. Obv: Nicaragua Coat of Arms. Rev: 1000 Cordobas, Liberty Bell, Philadelphia USA; 2000 Cordobas, Astronaut with American Flag Standing on Moon and Young Girl in US Colonial Dress Sewing Early American Flag.

NIGER

1. **10 Francs 1960**	....	**$900**
2. **25 Francs 1960**	....	**for**
3. **50 Francs 1960**	....	**the**
4. **100 Francs 1960**	....	**set**

Issued to commemorate the 5th Anniversary of Independence. Obv: President Hamani. Rev: Flags and Coat of Arms. Issued in 1967. All proofs. Considered NCLT.

5. **10 Francs 1968**	....	**$675**
6. **25 Francs 1968**	....	**for**
7. **50 Francs 1968**	....	**the**
8. **100 Francs 1968**	....	**set**

Obv: Coat of Arms. Rev: 10 Francs, Ostrich; 25, 50 and 100 Francs, Springbok.

Sizes and weights:
10 Francs, 18 mm, 3.2 gms 900 fine
25 Francs, 23 mm, 8 gms 900 fine
50 Francs, 28 mm, 16 gms 900 fine
100 Francs, 34 mm, 32 gms 900 fine

Mintages:
1960—1000 sets; 1968—

OMAN, (State of)

1. **50 Ryals 1971**	....	**$75**
2. **100 Ryals 1971**	....	**$90**
3. **200 Ryals 1971**	....	**$125**
4. **500 Ryals 1971**	....	**$300**

Obv: 50 Ryals, Dhow on Water; 100 Ryals, Flower; 200 Ryals, Falcon; 500 Ryals, Walled City. Rev: Cresent & Star, Crossed Flags, 2 Sabres and Date.

Sizes and weights:
50 Ryals, 20 mm, 4 gms 916²⁄₃ fine
100 Ryals, 23.5 mm, 8 gms 916²⁄₃ fine
200 Ryals, 28 mm, 16 gms 916²⁄₃ fine
500 Ryals, 45 mm, 40 gms 916²⁄₃ fine

Mintages:
2000 numbered sets plus; 50 Ryals—28,000; 100 Ryals—13,000; 200 Ryals—18,000; 500 Ryals—6000.

PANAMA

Announced: Series of 4 .900 fine coins for 1974, consisting of 25, 50, 100 and 200 Balboas. The 25 Balboas to be 16 mm 2.38 gms. The 50 Balboas, 21 mm and 4.76 gms. The 100 Balboas, 26 mm and 9.52 gms, and the 200 Balboas 36 mm and 19.04 gms.

PARAGUAY

1. 10,000 Guaranies 1968 . . . . **Rare**

Obv: Bust of Stroessner. Rev: Lion before Pole with Liberty Cap. A presentation piece, estimated 50 pieces struck. No records of sales or auctions. Coin has a lettered edge.

2. 1500 Guaranies 1972 . . . . $150
3. 3000 Guaranies 1972 . . . . $300
4. 4500 Guaranies 1972 . . . . $460

Obv: Uniformed Bust of General Stroessner. Rev: Star Surrounded by Wreath, Date and Denomination.

5. 1500 Guaranies 1973 . . . . $150
6. 3000 Guaranies 1973 . . . . $275
7. 4500 Guaranies 1973 . . . . $400

Issued to honor Alessandro Manzoni. Obv: Bust of Manzoni. Rev: Coat of Arms, Date, Denomination.

Sizes and weights:
1500 Guaranies, 25 mm, 10.62 gms 900 fine
3000 Guaranies, 32 mm, 21.25 gms, 900 fine
4500 Guaranies, 40 mm, 31.86 gms, 900 fine
10,000 Guaranies, 38 mm,   gms 900 fine

Mintages:
1965 Series—1500 each; 1973 Series—1500 each
10,000 Guaranies—50.

Announced: A coin set in 1974 to be issued to commemorate the 100th Anniversary of the Birth of Winston Churchill. 1500, 3000 and 4500 Guaranies. 1500 mintage of each. A silver 150 Guaranies Crown, 10,000 mintage will also be issued.

64

PERSIA (IRAN)

1. ½ Pahlevi 1932-6 .... $65

Obv: Head of Riza Khan Pahlevi. Rev: Lion.

2. ½ Pahlevi 1944-49 .... $45
3. 1 Pahlevi 1942-49 .... $85

Obv: Lion. Rev: Legend in Persian.

4. ¼ Pahlevi 1950-62 .... $25
5. ¼ Pahlevi 1950-62 (large planchet) ... $25
6. ½ Pahlevi 1950-62 .... $35
7. 1 Pahlevi 1950-62 .... $65
8. 1 Pahlevi 1950-62 (high relief) $85
9. 2½ Pahlevi 1962 .... $200
10. 5 Pahlevi 1962 .... $325

Obv: Head of Mohammed Riza Pahlevi. Rev: Lion.

11. 2½ Pahlevi 1960 .... $250

Obv: Head of Mohammed Riza Pahlevi. Rev: Inscription.

12. 5 Pahlevi 1961 .... $450

Obv: Bust of Shah & Wife, Farah Diba. Rev: Inscription

13. 500 Riyals 1972 .... $725
14. 750 Riyals 1972 .... for
15. 1000 Riyals 1972 .... the
16. 2500 Riyals 1972 .... set

Issued to commemorate the 2500th Anniversary of the Persian Empire. Obv: 2500 Riyals, Cojoined Heads of Shah and Empress; 1000 Riyals, Ruins; 750 Riyals, Cylinder of Cyrus; 500 Riyals, Griffin. Rev: Date, Denomination, Symbol of Empire and Legend. Five companion silver pieces. All proof. Considered NCLT.

Rev.

Sizes and weights:
¼ Pahlevi, 14.5 or 16 mm, 2.02 gms 900 fine
½ Pahlevi, 18 mm, 4.05 gms 900 fine
1 Pahlevi, 22 mm, 8.1 gms 900 fine
2½ Pahlevi, 30 mm, 20.3 gms 900 fine
5 Pahlevi, 40 mm, 40.6 gms 900 fine
500 Riyals, 21 mm, 6.51 gms 900 fine
750 Riyals, 26 mm, 9.77 gms 900 fine
1000 Riyals, 30 mm, 13.03 gms 900 fine
2500 Riyals, 40 mm, 26.06 gms 900 fine

Mintages:
¼ Pahlevi thru 5 Pahlevi—unknown; 500 Riyals—
11,500; 750 Riyals—   ; 1000 Riyals—
   ; 2500 Riyals—

PERU

1. 50 Soles 1967, 68, 69 . . . . **$500**

Obv: Head of Manco Capoc, Inca Chief. Rev:
Inca Crest. This is a restrike of a rare coin 1930,
1931. The original issued in 5000 pieces each of
2 years is valued at $1400. The 1969 piece is
rare—offered at $925, Sept. 1974.

2. 5 Soles 1956-64 . . . . **$30**
3. 10 Soles 1956-64 . . . . **$40**
4. 20 Soles 1950-64 . . . . **$75**
5. 50 Soles 1950-64 . . . . **$150**
6. 100 Soles 1950-64 . . . . **$375**

Obv: Liberty Seated. Rev: Coat of Arms. The
1952, and 1958 are rare. The 100 Soles were
issued to place gold on the market in Peru, to
satisfy demand of citizens.

PERU (cont.)

7. ⅕ Libra 1934-67 . . . . $25
8. ½ Libra 1934-69 . . . . $35
9. 1 Libra 1934-66 . . . . $60

Obv: Indian Head. Rev: Coat of Arms. A continuation of a series dating to 1898.

10. 50 Soles 1965 . . . . $350
11. 100 Soles 1965 . . . . $800

Issued to commemorate the 400th Anniversary of the Lima Mint. Obv: Copy of First Peruvian Coin. Rev: Coat of Arms and Denomination.

12. 50 Soles 1966 . . . . $350
13. 100 Soles 1966 . . . . $800

Issued to commemorate the victory over the Spanish in the Naval Battle of 1866. Obv: Winged Victory. Rev: Coat of Arms. A rare set, virtually never offered or auctioned.

Sizes and weights:

⅕ Libra, 14.5 mm, 1.59 gms 916⅔ fine
½ Libra, 19.3 mm, 3.99 gms 916⅔ fine
1 Libra, 22 mm, 7.98 gms 916⅔ fine
5 Soles, 15 mm, 2.34 gms 900 fine
10 Soles, 18 mm, 4.68 gms 900 fine
20 Soles, 23 mm, 9.36 gms 900 fine
50 Soles, 30 mm, 23.4 gms 900 fine
100 Soles, 37 mm, 46.8 gms 900 fine

Mintages:

⅕ Libra—Total 1958-67—159,479; ½ Libra—Total 1961-66—65,178; 1 Libra—Total 1959-69—72,104; 5 Soles—Total 1956-69—53,829; 10 Soles—Total 1956-69—39,848; 20 Soles—Total 1950-69—55,248; 50 Soles—Total 1950-69—61,011; 100 Soles—Total 1950-69—89,423; 50 Soles 1967—10,000, 1968—300; 50 Soles 1969—403; 1965—3000; 50 Soles 1966—3000; 100 Soles 1965—3000; 1966—3000.

PHILLIPINES

1. 1 Piso 1970 . . . . **est. $800**

Issued to commemorate visit of Pope Paul VI to the Phillipines. A rare presentation piece. There is a companion silver piece with 30,000 mintage and copper-nickel piece with 70,000 mintage. One gold piece appeared in an auction in 1972 and sold for $400. None heard of since on the market.

Size and weight:
30 mm, 19.7 gms 900 fine

Mintage:
1000

RAS AL KHAIMA

1. 50 Riyals 1970 . . . . $75
2. 75 Riyals 1970 . . . . $100
3. 100 Riyals 1970 . . . . $150
4. 150 Riyals 1970 . . . . $250
5. 200 Riyals 1970 . . . . $350

Issued to commemorate the founding of Rome as a city. Rev: Legend and Denomination. Obv: 50 Riyals, Map of Italy; 75 Riyals, City of Rome; 100 Riyals, Victory in World War I; 150 Riyals, Liberty Standing, A Wolf, Remus and Romulus; 200 Riyals, Romulus, Remus and Wolf. Considered NCLT. Three companion silver proof coins.

Sizes and weights:
50 Riyals, 24 mm, 10.35 gms 900 fine
75 Riyals, 28 mm, 15.53 gms 900 fine
100 Riyals, 31 mm, 20.7 gms 900 fine
150 Riyals, 34 mm, 31.5 gms 900 fine
200 Riyals, 40 mm, 41.4 gms 900 fine

Mintage:
2000 sets.

RHODESIA

1. ½ Pound 1966 . . . . $130
2. 1 Pound 1966 . . . . $210
3. 5 Pounds 1966 . . . . $750

Issued to commemorate first Anniversary of Independence. Obv: Bust of Queen Elizabeth II of Great Britain. Rev: ½ Pound, Antelope; 1 Pound, Lion and Elephant Tusk; 5 Pounds, Coat of Arms. Issued in proof .

Sizes and weights:
½ Pound, 18 mm, 3.99 gms 916²⁄₃ fine
1 Pound, 21 mm, 7.98 gms 916²⁄₃ fine
5 Pounds, 35 mm, 39.94 gms 916²⁄₃ fine

Mintages:
½ Pound—4000; 1 Pound—2000; 5 Pounds—1000.

ROUMANIA

1. **20 Lei 1939** **$300**
2. **100 Lei 1939** **$1750**

Obv: Head of Carol II. Rev: Coat of Arms.

3. **20 Lei 1939 (B)** **$300**

Obv: Head of Carol II. Rev: Shield and Eagle.

9. **150 Lei 1940** **$1300**

Issued to commemorate 10th Anniversary of Reign of King Carol II. Obv: King on Horseback. Rev: Farmer in Field Handing Water Vase to Woman. A rare coin. Sold at Hans Schulman Auction, New York, October 15, 1974 at above price.

4. **100 Lei 1939 (B)** **$1750**

Obv: Head of Carol II. Rev: Angel and Shield.

5. **20 Lei 1940** **$275**
6. **100 Lei 1940** **$1750**

Issued to commemorate 10th year of Reign of Carol II. Obv: Head of Carol II. Rev: Crown Over Emblem.

10. **20 Lei 1944** **$95**

Obv: Joined Heads of 3 Kings with Dates. Rev: Circle of Shields and Head of Eagle.

7. **20 Lei 1940 (B)** **$275**
8. **100 Lei 1940 (B)** **$1750**

Obv: Head and Legend. Rev: Word "Romania" and Crown Over Emblem.

ROUMANIA (cont.)

Sizes and weights:
20 Lei, 20 mm, 6.45 gms 900 fine
100 Lei, 34 mm, 32.25 gms 900 fine
150 Lei, 40 mm,   gms 900 fine

Mintages:
20 Lei 1939–   ; 1939 (B)–   ;
1940–   ; 1940 (B)–   ;
1944–74,480,000. 100 Lei 1939–   ; 1939
(B)–   ; 1940–   ; 1940 (B)–
150 Lei–

RWANDA

1. **10 Francs 1968** $675
2. **25 Francs 1968** . . . . for
3. **50 Francs 1968** . . . . the
4. **100 Francs 1968** . . . . set

Issued to commemorate the Independence of the Nation. Obv: Bust of President Kayibanda. Rev: Coat of Arms. All proof. Considered NCLT.

Sizes and weights:
10 Francs, 19 mm, 3.2 gms 900 fine
25 Francs, 23 mm, 8 gms 900 fine
50 Francs, 28 mm, 16 gms 900 fine
100 Francs, 34 mm, 32 gms 900 fine

Mintages:
10 Francs–10,000; 25 Francs–4,000; 50 Francs–3,000; 100 Francs–3,000.
There are 3000 sets issued from above mintages and the balance of 10 and 25 Francs coins shown here sold separately.

SAARLAND

1. **20 Francs 1954** . . . . **Rare**
2. **100 Francs 1955** . . . . **Rare**

Obv: 20 Fr. Design and Word Saarland in Circle; 100 Fr. Industrial Factory Design. Rev: 20 Fr. & 100 Fr., Date and Value.

Sizes and weights:
20 Francs, 23 mm, 4 gms 900 fine
100 Francs, 23 mm, 6 gms 900 fine

Mintages:
20 Francs–50; 100 Francs–50.

SALVADOR

1. **25 Colones 1971** $45
2. **50 Colones 1971** $75
3. **100 Colones 1971** $140
4. **200 Colones 1971** $300

Obv: 25C Fecundity; 50C Statue of Independence; 100C Americas; 200C Panchimalco Church. Rev: Coat of Arms of Salvador and Bust, (no bust on 50 Colones).

SALVADOR (cont.)

Sizes and weights:
25 Colones, 16 mm, 2.96 gms 900 fine
50 Colones, 23 mm, 5.9 gms 900 fine
100 Colones, 30 mm, 11.8 gms 900 fine
200 Colones, 38 mm, 23.6 gms 900 fine

Mintages:
25 Colones—7500; 50 Colones—   ; 100 Colones—   ; 200 Colones—

SAUDI ARABIA

1. **1 Pound 1951** **$80**

Obv: Arabic Legend. Rev: Arabic Legend.

2. **1 Pound 1957** **$90**

Obv: Crossed Sabres. Rev: Denomination.

Size and weight:
1 Pound, 20 mm, 7.98 gms 916²⁄₃ fine

Mintages:

Note: Also see United States of America, for special issues of 1945-6 by the U.S. Mint for use in Saudi Arabia.

SENEGAL

1. **10 Francs 1968** . . . . est. **$675**
2. **25 Francs 1968** . . . . for
3. **50 Francs 1968** . . . . the
4. **100 Francs 1968** . . . . set

Obv: Coat of Arms surrounded by Wreath. Rev: Denomination and Date. All proof. Considered NCLT.

Sizes and weights:
10 Francs, 18 mm, 3.2 gms 900 fine
25 Francs, 20 mm, 8 gms 900 fine
50 Francs, 28 mm, 16 gms 900 fine
100 Francs, 34 mm, 32 gms 900 fine

Mintages:

SHARJAH
(Emirate of)

1. **25 Riyals 1970** **$60**
2. **50 Riyals 1970** **$110**
3. **100 Riyals 1970** **$225**
4. **100 Riyals 1970 (B)** **$225**
5. **200 Riyals 1970** **$500**

Rev: Palm Tree and Crossed Flags. Obv: 25 Riyals, Mona Lisa; 50 Riyals, Jules Rimet Soccer Cup and World; 100 Riyals, Bust of Simon Bolivar; 100 Riyals (B), Bust of Napoleon; 200 Riyals, Head of Khalid bin Mohammed Al-Qasimi. Considered NCLT. Four silver proof companion pieces.

SHARJAH (Emirate of) (cont.)

Rev.

Sizes and weights:
25 Riyals, 21 mm, 5.18 gms 900 fine
50 Riyals, 28 mm, 10.36 gms 900 fine
100 Riyals, 35 mm, 20.73 gms 900 fine
200 Riyals, 50 mm, 41.46 gms 900 fine

Mintage:
5000 numbered sets

SIERRA LEONE

1. 1 Leone 1964 . . . . Rare
2. ¼ Golde 1966 . . . .$1000 for
3. ½ Golde 1966 . . . . .proof set, $750
4. 1 Golde 1966 . . . . .for unc set
5. ¼ Golde 1966 Palladium . . . . Rare
6. ½ Golde 1966 Palladium . . . . Rare
7. 1 Golde 1966 Palladium . . . . Rare

Issued to commemorate 5th Anniversary of Independence. Obv: Head of Lion. Rev: Map of Country and Denomination.

8. 1 Leone 1974 . . . . Rare

Issued to commemorate th 10th Anniversary of the Bank of Sierra Leone. Only 2 gold patterns were made by the Bank to present to the President, 38.66 mm.

Photo of companion silver piece

72

SIERRA LEONE (cont.)

Sizes and weights:
¼ Golde, 24 mm, 13.7 gms 900 fine
½ Golde, 32 mm, 27.4 gms 900 fine
1 Golde, 48 mm, 54.8 gms 900 fine
1 Leone,   mm,   gms 916²⁄₃ fine
(The proofs of the ¼, ½ and 1 Golde are
    916²⁄₃ fine)

Mintages:
1 Leone—12, ¼ Golde—proof—600 in 3 pc. set plus 400, unc—5000; ½ Golde—proof—600 in 3 pc. set plus 400, unc—2500; 1 Golde—proof—600, unc—1500; ¼, ½, 1 Golde in Palladium—100 sets. 1 Leone (1974)—2.

SINGAPORE

1. 150 Dollars 1969 . . . . **proof $250**
                                          BU $185

Obv: Coat of Arms. Rev: Raffles Lighthouse and Denomination.

Size and weight:
150 Dollars, 30.48 mm, 25 gms 920 fine

Mintages:
Proof—500; BU—28,500.

Announced: For 1975 a 100 Dollar silver, gold plated coin.

SOMALIA

1. 20 Shillings 1965	$60
2. 50 Shillings 1965	$85
3. 100 Shillings 1965	$120
4. 200 Shillings 1965	$250
5. 500 Shillings 1965	$600

Issued to commemorate the 5th Anniversary of Independence. Obv: Bust of Osman. Rev: Coat of Arms. Considered NCLT.

SOMALIA (cont.)

6. 20 Shillings 1970 . . . . $60
7. 50 Shillings 1970 . . . . $85
8. 100 Shillings 1970 . . . . $120
9. 200 Shillings 1970 . . . . $250
10. 500 Shillings 1970 . . . . $600

Issued to commemorate the 10th Anniversary of Independence. Obv. Coat of Arms. Rev: 20 Sh. Atomic Symbol; 50 Sh. Man and Vase; 100 Sh. Girl and Fruit; 200 Sh. Camel; 500 Sh. Building. Considered NCLT.

Obv.

11. 50 Shillings 1971 . . . . $8
12. 100 Shillings 1971 . . . . $12
13. 200 Shillings 1971 . . . . $22

Issued to commemorate 1st Anniversary of Revolution. Rev: Coat of Arms. Obv: 50 Sh. Lighthouse; 100 Sh. Palm Helmet and Gun; 10 Sh. Agricultural Scene.

Rev.

izes and weights:
0 Shillings, 18 mm, 2.8 gms 900 fine
0 Shillings, 23 mm, 7 gms 900 fine
00 Shillings, 28 mm, 14 gms 900 fine
00 Shillings, 38 mm, 28 gms 900 fine
00 Shillings, 48 mm, 70 gms 900 fine

Mintages:
965 Sets—6325; 1970 sets—8000; 1971 sets—

SOUTH AFRICA

South African Rands, ½ Rands and Kreuger-rands have and still are produced for profit, in the distribution of bullion. To this day the South African mint sells coins at 8% over spot value of gold. Proof coins however are generally numismatic.

1. ½ Pound 1952 proof $70
2. 1 Pound 1952 proof $100

Obv: Head of King George VI. Rev: Springbok

3. ½ Pound 1953-60 proof $80
4. 1 Pound 1953-60 proof $110

Obv: Head of Queen Elizabeth II of Great Britain. Rev: Springbok.

5. 1 Rand 1961- $40
6. 2 Rands 1961- $65

Obv: Head of Man; Rev: Springbok.

SOUTH AFRICA (cont.)

7. 1 Kreugerrand 1967- $165
Obv: Bust of Paul Kruger. Rev: Springbok.

Note: Kreugerrands are produced in proof condition also and sell at about 50-60% premium above the BU coins.

Sizes and weights:
½ Pound, 18 mm, 3.99 gms 916²⁄₃ fine
1 Pound, 21 mm, 7.98 gms 916²⁄₃ fine
1 Rand, 18 mm, 3.99 gms 916²⁄₃ fine
2 Rands, 21 mm, 7.98 gms 916²⁄₃ fine
1 Kreugerrand, 31 mm, 33.19 gms 916²⁄₃ fine

Mintages:
½ Pound 1952—16,002; 1953—4000; 1954—850; 1955—300; 1957—380; 1958—360; 1959—1130; 1960—3002.
1 Pound 1952—16,502; 1953—3000; 1954—850; 1955—300; 1957—380; 1958—360; 1959—1132; 1960—3111.
1 Rand 1961—8178; 1962—6299; 1963—6531; 1964—9866; 1965—10,232; 1966—10,005; 1967—10,053; 1968—10,034; 1969—10,000; 1970—17,000.
2 Rands—1961—6946; 1962—12,344; 1963—5687; 1964—7994; 1965—10,366; 1966—10,011; 1967—10,169; 1968—9375; 1969—10,000; 1970—17,000.

Announced: Possible issuance of ¼ and ½ Kreugerrands (¼ and ½ oz. of gold) in 1975 to satisfy the demand for gold bullion in the United States when legal to hold.

SOUTH KOREA

1. 1000 Won 1970	. . . .	.$5⬤
2. 2500 Won 1970	. . . .	$10⬤
3. 5000 Won 1970	. . . .	$20⬤
4. 10,000 Won 1970	. . . .	$40⬤
5. 20,000 Won 1970	. . . .	$75⬤
6. 25,000 Won 1970	. . . .	$90⬤

Rev: Coat of Arms. Obv: 1000 Won, Great South Gate; 2500 Won, Queen Sunduk; 5000 Won, Turtle Ship; 10,000 Won, President Chung Hee Park; 20,000 Won, Crown of Silla Dynasty; 25,000 Won, King Sejong. Considered NCLT. Companion set of 6 silver proof coins

SOUTH KOREA (cont.)

Rev.

Sizes and weights:
1000 Won, 18 mm, 3.87 gms 900 fine
2500 Won, 26 mm, 9.68 gms 900 fine
5000 Won, 32 mm, 19.36 gms 900 fine
10,000 Won, 40 mm, 38.72 gms 900 fine
20,000 Won, 55 mm, 77.44 gms 900 fine
25,000 Won, 60 mm, 96.8 gms 900 fine

Mintages:
4500 numbered sets.

SPAIN

1. 10 Pesetas (1878) $45
2. 20 Pesetas (1887) (1896) $55
3. 25 Pesetas (1876) $85
4. 100 Pesetas (1897) $450

Obv: 10 Pesetas, Young Head of Alfonso XII;
20 Pesetas (1887), Baby Head Alfonso XIII; 20
Pesetas (1896), Boys Head Alfonso XIII; 25
Pesetas, Older Head with Beard Alfonso XII;
100 Pesetas, Boys Head Alfonso XIII. Reverse
on all: Coat of Arms.

SPAIN (cont.)

Sizes and weights:
20 Pesetas, 20 mm, 6.4 gms 900 fine
25 Pesetas, 23 mm, 8.06 gms 900 fine
100 Pesetas, 33 mm, 32.2 gms 900 fine
10 Pesetas, 18 mm, 3.22 gms 900 fine

Mintages:
Restrikes—Unknown.

Note: No Spanish Coins have been issued since 1934. However, several older pieces have been officially restruck in 1961 and 1962. To tell original from restrikes, look at stars on each side of old date. The original will (for example) have the number "18" and "80" in the two stars. The restrike "19" and "62".

SWAZILAND

1. 1 Lilangeni 1968 . . . . est. $650

Issued to commemorate Independence. Obv: Head of King Sobhuza II. Rev: Coat of Arms. This is a rare coin due to its mintage and use as a presentation piece. There is a companion 5 piece proof set in silver of 10,000 mintage.

2. 5 Emalangeni 1974 . . . . est. $575
3. 10 Emalangeni 1974 . . . . for
4. 20 Emalangeni 1974 . . . . the
5. 25 Emalangeni 1974 . . . . set

Issued to commemorate the 75th Anniversary of Birth of King Sobhuza II. Obv: Face of King Sobhuza II. Rev: 5 Emalangeni, Coat of Arms; 10 Emalangeni Swazi Maiden in Traditional Dress; 20 Emalangeni, Emblem of UNICEF and Swazi Child in Traditional Dress; 25 Emalangeni, Queen Mother Gwamile and the King as a young boy. The 10 Emalangeni is scalloped, and the 20 Emalangeni is 10 sided.

Obv.

SWAZILAND (cont.)

Size and weight:
1 Lilangeni, 33 mm, 33.39 gms 916²/₃ fine
5 Emalangeni, 22 mm, 5.56 gms 900 fine
10 Emalangeni, 26 mm, 11.12 gms 900 fine
20 Emalangeni, 34 mm, 22.24 gms 900 fine
25 Emalangeni, 38 mm, 27.8 gms 900 fine

Mintages:
1 Lilangeni—2000; 1974 Series—15,000 sets. Plus 45,000 of the 5 Emalangeni; 25,000 of the 10 Emalangeni; 10,000 of the 20 Emalangeni.

3. 25 Francs 1955,8,9 . . . . *
4. 50 Francs 1955,8,9 . . . . *

Obv: 25 Fr., William Tell with Crossbow; 50 Fr., 3 Figures Standing. Rev: Value and Date.

Sizes and weights:
100 Francs 1934, 30 mm, 25.9 gms 900 fine
100 Francs 1939, 26 mm, 17.5 gms 900 fine
25 Francs, 23 mm, 5.64 gms 900 fine
50 Francs, 18 mm, 11.29 gms 900 fine

Mintages:
100 Francs 1934—2000; 100 Francs 1939—6000; 25 Francs—5,000,000 each year; 50 Francs—2,000,000 each year.

*The 25 and 50 Franc pieces were never released.

SWITZERLAND

1. 100 Francs 1934 . . . . **$2300**

Issued to commemorate Fribourg Shooting Festival. Obv: Standing Rifleman. Rev: Oval Shield and Denomination. A rare coin.

SYRIA

1. ½ Pound 1950 . . . . **$120**
2. 1 Pound 1950 . . . . **$100**

Obv: Eagle. Rev: Legend within Rectangle.

2. 100 Francs 1939 . . . . **$1100**

Issued to commemorate the Lucerne Shooting Festival. Obv: Kneeling Rifleman. Rev: Legend, Shield and Denomination. A scarce coin.

Sizes and weights:
½ Pound, 18 mm, 3.37 gms 900 fine
1 Pound, 20 mm, 6.75 gms 900 fine

Mintages:
½ Pound—100,000; 1 Pound—250,000.

TANGIER

1 Hercules (ND) **$325**

Issued in 1954 by N.M. Rothschild & Sons, a private bank as a bullion coin. Obv: Hercules Standing. Rev: Weight and Refiners Name.

Size and weight:
1 Hercules, 25 mm, 1 Troy Oz. 916²⁄₃ fine

Mintage :
Unknown

TANZANIA

Announced: 1500 Shillings; part of Conservation Coin Series. Obv: Head of President Julius K. Nyerere. Rev: Cheetah, 34 mm, 33.4 gms, 900 fine. Issue in 10,000 unc and 3,000 proofs. Two companion silver pieces.

THAILAND

1. **20 Ticals 1935-46** **$500**
2. **200 Ticals 1935-46** **$1250**

Emergency coins struck to make government gold available to the public just before Japanese invasion of World War II. Obv: Garuda Bird. Rev: 2 Line Legend. Rare. Values from 1973 and 1974 Auctions.

3. **150 Bahts 1968** **$275**
4. **300 Bahts 1968** .... for
5. **600 Bahts 1968** .... the set

Issued to honor the 36th Birthday of Queen Sirikit. Obv: Bust of Queen. Rev: Queen's Initials.

6. **400 Bahts 1972** .... **$300 for**
7. **800 Bahts 1972** .... the set

Issued to commemorate the 25 Anniversary of the reign of King. Obv: Bust of King. Rev: Design.

THAILAND (cont.)

Sizes and weights:
50 Baht, 16 mm, 3.69 gms 900 fine
300 Baht, 20 mm, 7.32 gms 900 fine
400 Baht, 22 mm, 14.93 gms 900 fine
500 Baht, 26 mm, 9.91 gms 900 fine
800 Baht, 30 mm, 20.08 gms 900 fine
20 Ticals, 26 mm, 14 gms 996 fine
200 Ticals, 42 mm, 140 gms 996 fine

Mintages:*
20 Ticals—Unknown; 200 Ticals—Unknown;
1968 Series—20,000 Sets; 1972 Series—20,000
Sets.
*Mintages unconfirmed.

Announced: A 2500 Baht coin part of the
Conservation Coin Series. Obv: King Bhumibol
Adulyadej. Rev: The White-eyed River Martin,
54 mm, 33.4 gms .900 fine. Issued in 10,000
uncs and 3000 proofs. Two silver companion
coins.

TONGA

1. ¼ Koula 1962 .... $100
2. ½ Koula 1962 .... $150
3. 1 Koula 1962 .... $700

Rev: Coat of Arms. Obv: ¼ Koula, Bust of
Queen Salote Tupou III, ½ and 1 Koula,
Standing Figure of Queen. Proofs valued at 50%
above UNCS.

Rev.

TONGA (cont.)

4. ¼ Koula 1962 Platinum . . . . . est. $4000
5. ½ Koula 1962 Platinum . . . . . for
6. 1 Koula 1962 Platinum . . . . . the set

Same description as above. Exceedingly Rare.

7. ¼ Hau 1967 Palladium . . . . . est. $750
8. ½ Hau 1967 Palladium . . . . . for
9. 1 Hau 1967 Palladium . . . . . . the set

Issued to commemorate the Kings Coronation. Obv: Bust of King Taufa'ahau Tupou IV. Rev: Coat of Arms. A rare set.

10. ¼ Hau 1968 Palladium . . . . . est. $900
11. ½ Hau 1968 Palladium . . . . . for
12. 1 Hau 1968 Palladium . . . . . . the set

Issued to commemorate the Kings 50th Birth day. Obv: Bust of King Taufa'ahau Tupou IV Rev: Coat of Arms. A rare set. The 196 Palladium set is identical to the 1967 Palladium set except for a counterstamp on the observ (see illustration).

Obv.

Counterstamp

Sizes and weights:

¼ Koula, 20 mm, 8.12 gms $916^{2/3}$ fine
½ Koula, 30 mm, 16.25 gms $916^{2/3}$ fine
1 Koula, 45 mm, 32.5 gms $916^{2/3}$ fine
¼ Hau, 24 mm, 16 gms 980 fine*
½ Hau, 33 mm, 32 gms 980 fine*
1 Hau, 47 mm, 63.5 gms 980 fine*
The 1962 proof sets are reportedly pure gol

*The palladium pieces have the following conte 98% Palladium and 2% Ruthenium.

Mintages:

¼ Koula—proof—450, BU—3500 + 1500 in se
½ Koula—proof—350, BU—3000 + 1500 in se
1 Koula—proof—250, BU—1500 all in se
Platinum set 1962—25 sets; 1967 Palladiu
set—400 sets + 37 pieces of ½ Hau and 20
pieces of ¼ Hau. 1968 Palladium set—150
sets + 113 pieces of ½ Hau.

TUNIS
(TUNISIA)

1. 100 Francs 1930-37 . . . . **$140**

Obv: Arabic Legend. Rev. Denomination and Date.

2. 100 Francs 1938-1955 . . . . est. **$400**

Obv: Arabic Legend. Rev: Date, No Denomination. Rare coins. Only about 30 pieces reported minted each year.

3. 2 Dinars 1967 . . . . **$1800**
4. 5 Dinars 1967 . . . . **for**
5. 10 Dinars 1967 . . . . **the**
6. 20 Dinars 1967 . . . . **set**
7. 40 Dinars 1967 . . . .

Issued to commemorate the 10th Anniversary of the Republic. Obv: Head of President Habib Bourguiba. Rev: Minaret. Considered NCLT.

Sizes and weights:
100 Francs, 21 mm, 6.5 gms 900 fine
2 Dinars,   mm, 3.8 gms 900 fine
5 Dinars,   mm, 9.5 gms 900 fine
10 Dinars,   mm, 19 gms 900 fine
20 Dinars,   mm, 38 gms 900 fine
40 Dinars,   mm, 76 gms 900 fine

Mintages:
100 Francs (1930-7)— ; 100 Francs (1938-55)—About 30 each year; 2 Dinars—7259; 5 Dinars—7259; 10 Dinars—4480; 20 Dinars—3536; 40 Dinars—3031.
There were 3031 sets issued and the balance of the 2,5,10 and 20 Dinars listed above were sold individually.

TURKEY

Series (A)
1. 25 Piastres 1943- $35
2. 50 Piastres 1943- $55
3. 100 Piastres 1943- $90
4. 250 Piastres 1943- $150
5. 500 Piastres 1943- $300

Obv: Head of President Kemal Ataturk. Rev: Legend and Date. The date 1923 appears on all coins plus a 2nd number. Add 23 to the number to get the date of mintage.

Series (B)
6. 25 Piastres 1942-51,60-73 . . . . $35
7. 50 Piastres 1942-51,60-73 . . . . $55
8. 100 Piastres 1942-51,57,59 . . . . $90
9. 250 Piastres 1942-51,60-73 . . . . . . $150
10. 500 Piastres 1942-51,60-73 . . . . . . $300

So called deluxe coins. Obv: Head of Ataturk in Circle of Stars, and Circle of Elaborate Oriental Design. Rev: Legend plus actual date. Prooflike in appearance.

Series (C)
11. 25 Piastres 1943-9 . . . . $35
12. 50 Piastres 1943-9 . . . . $55
13. 100 Piastres 1943-9 . . . . $90
14. 250 Piastres 1943-9 . . . . $150
15. 500 Piastres 1943-9 . . . . $300

Obv: Head of President Ismat Inonu. Rev: Legend and Date (Same 1923, plus other number system as 1-5 Above)

Series (D)
16. 25 Piastres 1944-7 . . . . $35
17. 50 Piastres 1944-7 . . . . $55
18. 100 Piastres 1944-7 . . . . $90
19. 250 Piastres 1944-7 . . . . $150
20. 500 Piastres 1944-7 . . . . $300

So called deluxe coins. Obv: Head of Inonu in Circle of Stars, and Circle of Elaborate Oriental Design. Rev: Legend Plus Actual Date. Proof like in appearance.

TURKEY (cont.)

21. 500 Lira 1973 . . . . $85

Obv: Bust of President. Rev: Shooting Star with Tail, Legend and Date.

Sizes and weights:
25 Piastres, 14.75 mm, 1.8 gms 916²⁄₃ fine
50 Piastres, 18.0 mm, 3.6 gms 916²⁄₃ fine
100 Piastres, 22.0 mm, 7.2 gms 916²⁄₃ fine
250 Piastres, 27.2 mm, 18.0 gms 916²⁄₃ fine
500 Piastres, 35.0 mm, 36.0 gms 916²⁄₃ fine
25 Piastres deluxe, 18 mm, 1.75 gms 916²⁄₃ fine
50 Piastres deluxe, 22.5 mm, 3.5 gms 916²⁄₃ fine
100 Piastres deluxe, 31 mm, 7.0 gms 916²⁄₃ fine
250 Piastres deluxe, 40 mm, 17.5 gms 916²⁄₃ fine
500 Piastres deluxe, 46 mm, 35 gms 916²⁄₃ fine
500 Lira (1973), 22 mm, 6 gms 916²⁄₃ fine

Mintages:
25 Piastres Series (A) 932,369, (B) 1,016,147, (C) 96,628, (D) 2,467; 50 Piastres Series (A) 284,273, (B) 565,202, (C) 28,710, (D) 5,602; 100 Piastres Series (A) 4,238,649, (B) 2,039,392, (C) 458,117, (D) 53,269; 250 Piastres Series (A) 17,485, (B) 2,406,467, (C) 24,525, (D) 87,132; 500 Piastres Series (A) 55,613, (B) 56,051, (C) 28,734, (D) 6,576.

TURKS AND CALICOS ISLANDS

Announced: A 100 Crown to be issued in 1975 to commemorate the 100th Anniversary of the Birth of Winston Churchill. A 20 Crown silver companion piece will also be issued.

This photo is of the silver 20 Crown—the 100 Crown Gold Design is the same but photo unavailable.

UGANDA

1. 50 Shillings 1969 . . . . $75
2. 100 Shillings 1969 . . . . $125
3. 500 Shillings 1969 . . . . $600
4. 1000 Shillings 1969 . . . . $1100

Rev: Coat of Arms. Obv: 50 Sh., Martyr's Shrine; 100 Sh., Pope Paul VI and Map of Africa; 500 Sh., Pope Paul VI and Globe; 1000 Sh., Bust of Pope Paul VI. Considered NCLT. Companion set of 6 silver proof coins.

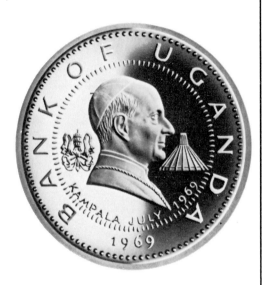

Rev.

Sizes and weights:
50 Shillings, 21 mm, 6.91 gms 900 fine
100 Shillings, 30 mm, 13.82 gms 900 fine
500 Shillings, 53 mm, 69.12 gms 900 fine
1000 Shillings, 60 mm, 138.24 gms 900 fine

Mintages:
3000 numbered sets.

UM AL QAWAIN
(Emirate of)

1. **25 Riyals 1970** **$70**
2. **50 Riyals 1970** **$125**
3. **100 Riyals 1970** **$250**
4. **200 Riyals 1970** **$500**

Obv: 25 R, Cannon; 50 R, Castle; 100 R, Gazelles; 200 R., Emir Bin Rashid Almoalla. All proofs. Considered NCLT. Four companion silver pieces.

Rev.

Sizes and weights:
25 Riyals, 21 mm, 5.18 gms 900 fine
50 Riyals, 28 mm, 10.36 gms 900 fine
100 Riyals, 35 mm, 20.73 gms 900 fine
200 Riyals, 50 mm, 41.46 gms 900 fine

Mintages:
5000 of each.

UNITED STATES OF AMERICA

Yes, such coins do exist. Produced in the Philadelphia Mint in 1945-6 for use by a U.S. Company in Saudi Arabia, where payment was required in gold. These "discs" of gold used as money and are considered coins by many and are numismatic collectibles. See Friedberg, "Gold Coins of the World," Third Ed., page 385, Fr. #107, 108. Coins are rare, most reportedly melted.

1. 1 Pound ND **$350**
2. 4 Pounds ND **$550**

Obv: U.S. Eagle and Legend "U.S. Mint, Philadelphia USA". Rev: 3 incuse Lines with Wording Indicating fineness & weight.

Sizes and weights:
1 Pound, 21 mm, .2534 oz. 916²⁄₃ fine
4 Pound, 30 mm, 493 grains 916²⁄₃ fine

Mintages: *
1 Pound—9000; 4 Pounds—12,000.

*Unconfirmed

URUGUAY

1. 1 Centisimo 1953 . . . . **Rare**
2. 2 Centisimo 1953 . . . . **Rare**
3. 5 Centisimo 1953 . . . . **Rare**
4. 10 Centisimo 1953 . . . . **Rare**

Gold presentation set of 4 coins. See "Modern World Coins" by Yeoman (Y28-31).

5. 1 Peso 1968 . . . . **Rare**
6. 5 Peso 1968 . . . . **Rare**
7. 10 Peso 1968 . . . . **Rare**
8. 20 Peso 1968 . . . . **Rare**
9. 50 Peso 1968 . . . . **Rare**

Gold presentation set of 5 coins. 1, 5, 10, 20, 50 Pesos (Y42-44,51,52).

URUGUAY (cont.)

10. 1 Peso 1969 . . . . **Rare**
11. 5 Peso 1969 . . . . **Rare**
12. 10 Peso 1969 . . . . **Rare**

Gold presentation set of 3 coins, 1, 5, 10 Peso (Y48-50).

Sizes and weights:
See Yeoman's "Modern Coins of the World" for sizes. Uruguay coins generally minted in gold are .916²/₃ fine.

Mintages:
1953 set—100 sets; 1968 set—50 sets; 1969 set—50 sets.

Note: A special set of 3 gold 10 Centavos, 20 Centavos and 5 Peso (of 1930). Commemorative Issue was issued in proof in 1959. 60 sets in the Paris Mint. Sold in June 1973 auction @ $1450.00.

VATICAN CITY

1. 100 Lire 1933-34,35 . . . . **$300**

Issued to commemorate the Holy Year—both dates on coin. Obv: Bust of Pope Pius XI. Rev: Christ Standing. The 1935 a Regular issue.

2. 100 Lire 1936,7 (Size Reduced) **$375**
Obv: Bust of Pope Pius XI. Rev: Christ Standing.

3. 100 Lire 1939-41 . . . . **$500**
Obv: Bust of Pope Pius XII. Rev: Christ Standing.

4. 100 Lire 1942-49 . . . . **$400**
Obv: Bust of Pope Pius XII. Rev: Charity Seated with Children. 1948,9 rare dates.

5. 100 Lire 1950 . . . . **$270**
Issued to commemorate 1950 Holy Year. Obv: Crowned Bust of Pope Pius XII. Rev: Opening of Holy Door.

89

VATICAN CITY (cont.)

6. 100 Lire 1951-6 . . . . **$600**

Obv: Bust of Pope Pius XII. Rev: Charity Standing.

7. 100 Lire 1957-8 . . . . **$450**

Obv: Bust of Pope Pius XII. Rev: Coat of Arms.

8. 100 Lire 1959 . . . . **$3000**

Obv: Bust of Pope John XXIII. Rev: Coat of Arms.

Sizes and weights:
100 Lire 1933-5, 23.5 mm, 8.79 gms 900 fine
100 Lire 1936-59, 20.5 mm, 5.2 gms 900 fine

Mintages:
100 Lire—1933-4—23,235; 1934—2533;
1935—7015; 1936—8239; 1937—2000;
1938—1; 1939—2100; 1940—2000;
1941—2000; 1942—2000; 1943—1000;
1944—1000; 1945—1000; 1946—1000;
1947—1000; 1948—5000; 1949—1000;
1950—4000; 1951—1000; 1952—1000;
1953—1000; 1954—1000; 1955—1000;
1956—1000; 1957—2000; 1958—3000;
1959—3000.

YEMEN

1. ¼ Imadi 1947, 1951-8 . . . . **$300**
2. ½ Imadi 1951 . . . . **$400**
3. 1 Imadi 1958 . . . . **$900**

Obv: Inscription with Crescent Symbol. Rev: Arabic Inscription.

YEMEN (cont.)

4. 5 Ryals 1969 . . . . $80
5. 10 Ryals 1969 . . . . $150
6. 20 Ryals 1969(A) $150
7. 20 Ryals 1969 (B) $150
8. 30 Ryals 1969 . . . . $225
9. 50 Ryals 1969 . . . . $500

Obv: Coat of Arms. Rev: 5 Ryals. Head of Falcon; 10 Ryals, Gazelles; 20 Ryals (A) Camel; 20 Ryals (B) Apollo 11 Moon Landing; 30 Ryals Head of Azzubain; 50 Ryals Lion. All proof. Considered NCLT. Two companion pieces in silver proofs.

Sizes and weights:
¼ Imadi, 23 mm, 7.62 gms 900 fine
½ Imadi, 30 mm, 15.23 gms 900 fine
1 Imadi, 39 mm, 30.45 gms 900 fine
5 Ryals, 20 mm, 4.9 gms 900 fine
10 Ryals, 26 mm, 9.8 gms 900 fine
20 Ryals, 32 mm, 19.6 gms 900 fine
30 Ryals, 36 mm, 29.4 gms 900 fine
50 Ryals, 46 mm, 49 gms 900 fine

Mintages:
5 Ryals—2000; 10 Ryals—   ; 20 Ryals—
    ; 30 Ryals—   ; 50 Ryals—
Imadi Series—unknown.

YUGOSLAVIA

1. 100 Dinars 1968 . . . . **$110**
2. 500 Dinars 1968 . . . . **$450**

Obv: People with Flags, View of Town of Jajce.
Rev: Coat of Arms. One companion silver
piece, 20 Dinars.

3. 200 Dinars 1968 . . . . **$185**
4. 1000 Dinars 1968 . . . . **$850**

Issued to commemorate 25th Anniversary of
Council of National Liberation. Obv: Bust of
President Tito. Rev: Coat of Arms. One com-
panion silver piece, 50 Dinars.

Sizes and weights:
100 Dinars, 23 mm, 7.82 gms 900 fine
200 Dinars, 30 mm, 15.64 gms 900 fine
500 Dinars, 45 mm, 39.1 gms 900 fine
1000 Dinars, 55 mm. 78.2 gms 900 fine

Mintages:
10,000 of each authorized. Actual mintage
unknown.

CARE OF GOLD COINS

Owning Gold Coins leads to a responsibility to yourself and to your investment (which often becomes sizable), therefore, carefully consider these following recommendations:

1. *Handling of Coins:*

Always limit the handling of gold coins. When you do so, hold the coin by its edge between your fingertips, or with soft cotton gloves. DO NOT put fingers on the surface of the coin, as body acids can damage the coin. Gold is soft; be careful as you may scratch the surface. Gold coins also can easily be bent.

2. *Cleaning:*

If a coin is dirty, either leave it that way or remove heavy dirt with a soft cotton swab and alcohol. Pat, do not wipe the coin dry again with soft cotton cloth. Coins tone with age, which adds to their appearance and desirability. Cleaning will remove or alter the toning, which may reduce the value of the coin. Some electronic coin cleaning devices have been developed, but have not yet tested and cannot, therefore be recommended.

3. *Storage:*

Coins should be stored in clear, inert plastic envelopes and any identification or information can be written on self-adhering outside stickers. Equally as good is the use of 2 x 2's, with their plastic or cellophane circular viewing area, surrounded by cardboard on which information can be written. If the coin is larger than U.S. half dollar, put it first in a plastic envelope, cut off the flap, and then staple the envelope into a 2 x 2. This will hold the coin firm and protect its larger surface. (The large area 2 x 2's tend to tear.) The plastic envelopes and/or 2 x 2's can be stored in (2" x 2" x 9") boxes, readily available from dealers and supply houses, or can be placed in albums.

4. *Security:*

A gold coin Collection is valuable and will be a ready target if you are burglarized. It represents a lot of money in a very small, portable unit. Therefore, arrange a safe place to store coins. Best, of course, is a safe deposit box in a bank. This has a detriment, inability to view or show your collection, except at the bank. Next best is a home safe, a fire-resistant insulated one . . . otherwise your coins may, after a fire, end up as bullion. Get a safe sufficient to hold at least four 2" x 2" x 9" boxes and weighing 100 pounds or more. Label it outside "Papers only stored inside". It may fool a burglar who will not waste his time on opening the safe. If you are transporting coins, be careful with them. Count them when you take them out, and return them to the safe.

Keep an inventory up-to-date, and in a safe place, other than with the coins. This can be valuable for insurance purposes, if a loss occurs.

A word on Insurance. Most fire and theft policies include coin an/or stamp collections only with a nominal limit of $250 or thereabouts. If your collection is valuable, insure it under a "Personal Articles Floater", if your premiums are not excessive. Otherwise, contact the American Numismatic Association in Colorado Springs, Colorado, which has an insurance plan for its members.

5. *Repairs:*

Coins which have been holed, mounted or otherwise purposely or accidentally damaged can be repaired. But . . . a repaired coin will always be a repaired coin, and its value less than a quality condition coin. If you have damaged coins, use a skilled repairman. Often you will have to wait 3-6 months for work to be completed, but it will be worth it, as the coin, if enhanced, will at least become a more collectible and more valuable type piece than before.

POPULAR BULLION COINS

with intrinsic gold values
in U.S. Dollars

Gold Price Per Ounce	$150	$160	$170	$180	$190	$200
U.S. $20 .900 Fine	145.13	154.80	164.48	174.15	183.82	193.49
Austria 1 Ducat .986 Fine	16.61	17.71	18.82	19.93	21.04	22.15
Austria 4 Ducat .986 Fine	66.85	70.83	75.26	79.69	84.10	88.51
Austria 10 Francs .900 Fine	14.00	14.93	15.86	16.79	17.72	18.65
Austria 20 Francs .900 Fine	28.01	29.87	31.74	33.61	35.48	37.35
Austria 10 Corona .900 Fine	14.70	15.68	16.66	17.64	18.62	19.60
Austria 20 Corona .900 Fine	29.40	31.36	33.32	35.28	37.24	39.16
Austria 100 Corona .900 Fine	147.03	156.83	166.63	176.44	186.25	196.06
British Sovereign .9167 Fine	35.31	37.66	40.02	42.37	44.72	47.07
Columbia 5 Peso .9167 Fine	35.31	37.66	40.02	42.37	44.72	47.07
France 20 Francs .900 Fine	28.01	29.87	31.74	33.61	35.48	37.35
Hungary 10 Korona .900 Fine	14.70	15.68	16.66	17.64	18.62	19.60
Hungary 20 Korona .900 Fine	29.40	31.36	33.32	35.28	37.24	39.16
Hungary 100 Korona .900 Fine	147.03	156.83	166.63	176.44	186.25	196.06
Mexico 2 Peso .900 Fine	7.23	7.71	8.19	8.68	9.17	9.66
Mexico 2½ Peso .900 Fine	9.05	9.65	10.25	10.85	11.45	12.05
Mexico 5 Pesos .900 Fine	18.08	19.28	20.49	21.69	22.89	24.09
Mexico 10 Pesos .900 Fine	36.17	38.58	40.99	43.40	45.81	48.22
Mexico 20 Pesos .900 Fine	72.33	77.15	81.97	86.80	91.63	96.46
Mexico 50 Pesos .900 Fine	180.84	192.90	204.95	217.01	229.07	241.13
Russia 5 Roubles .900 Fine	18.68	19.92	21.17	22.41	23.65	24.89
Russia 10 Roubles .900 Fine	37.34	39.82	42.31	44.80	47.29	49.78
S.Af. Kruggerrand .9167 Fine	150.00	160.00	170.00	180.00	190.00	200.00
Switz. 20 Francs .900 Fine	28.01	29.87	31.74	33.61	35.48	37.35
Turkey 500 Piastres .9167 Fine	159.53	170.16	180.80	191.43	202.06	212.69

COUNTRIES HAVING ANNOUNCED
NEW GOLD ISSUES

Bahamas
Bangladesh*
Belize
Cambodia
Cayman Islands
Colombia*
Cook Islands
Costa Rica*
Ecuador*
El Salvador*
Ethiopia*
Falkland Islands
Fiji Islands
Haiti
Iceland*
Indonesia*

Jamaica*
Jordan*
Mauritius*
Mongolia*
Morocco*
Nepal*
Nicaragua
Pakistan*
Panama
Paraguay
South Africa
Tanzania*
Thailand*
Turks & Calicos Islands
Venezuela*

*Denotes countries participating in the Conservation Coin Series which have been announced.

Note: The most ambitious International numismatic undertaking ever has just been announced. Call the Conservation Coin Series it will include not less than 24 nations, each issuing two silver and one gold coin, in both proof and uncirculated condition. Each coin will depict a rare or endangered species of wildlife. Six nations have already announced their coin designs. There are 18 countries with whom the sponsors of the Conservation Coin series are still negotiating. These nations have yet to be announced and full information will be included when announced in the Newsletter Service offered on the last page of this catalog. Those countries not as yet having published designs for Conservation Coins do not appear in the body of this catalog.

Official Government Gold Restrikes

AUSTRIA

1892 4 Florins (10 Francs)

1892 8 Florins (20 Francs)

1915 1 Ducat

1915 4 Ducats

1892 10 Kronen

1912 10 Kronen

1892 20 Kronen

1915 20 Kronen

1915 100 Kronen

FRANCE

1907-1914 20 Francs (Restruck between 1951-1957 and in 1974)

GREAT BRITAIN

1925 Sovereign (Restruck between 1949-1951)

HUNGARY

1907 100 Korona Coronation (UP to right of date)

1892 20 Korona

1892 10 Korona

1870 8 Forint (Small head)

1870 4 Forint (small head)

1890 8 Forint (large head)

1890 4 Forint (small head)

1868 1 Ducat (standing king)

1880 1 Ducat

INDIA

1835 2 Mohur

1835 1 Mohur

1862 1 Mohur

1870 1 Mohur

1878 1 Mohur

1879 1 Mohur

1862 10 Rupees

1878 10 Rupees

1870 5 Rupees

1879 5 Rupees

1918 15 Rupees

LIECHTENSTEIN

1728 Ducat

1758 Ducat

1778 Ducat

1616 10 Ducats

1728 10 Ducats

(All Liechtenstein restrikes contain small letter M.)

MEXICO
Gold Restrikes

1945 2 Pesos

1945 2½ Pesos

1955 5 Pesos

1959 20 Pesos

1947 50 Pesos

SPAIN

1878 10 Pesetas (Restrike date 1961 in stars either side of date 1878)

1887 20 Pesetas (Restruck 1961)

1896 20 Pesetas (Restruck 1961)

SPAIN

1887 20 Pesetas (Restruck 1962)

1876 25 Pesetas (Restruck 1962)

1897 100 Pesetas (Restrike dates 1961 or 1962 in stars on either side of date 1897)

SWITZERLAND

1935 20 Francs (Restruck 1945-1949, L close to date)

1947 20 Francs; edge AD LEGEM MCMXXXI

TURKEY

1923 500 Piastres

1923 250 Piastres

1923 100 Piastres

1923 50 Piastres

1923 25 Piastres

(Note: 1923 is ascension year; year of striking is given in number below date—add the number to 1923 to get proper year)

WEIGHTS AND MEASURES

Purity:

24 carats	=	1000 fine (pure gold)
22 carats	=	$916^{2/3}$ fine
21 19/32 carats	=	900 fine
21 carats	=	875 fine
18 carats	=	750 fine
14 carats	=	$583^{1/3}$ fine
1 carat	=	41.67 fine

Weights:

1 Troy oz.	=	31.103 grams
1 Troy oz.	=	480 grains
32.15 oz.	=	1000 grams (1 kilogram)
1 grain	=	0.0648 grams
1 gram	=	0.643 pennyweight
1000 grams	=	1 kilogram
1 Troy oz.	=	20 pennyweight
1 Avoirdupois oz.	=	28.34 grams
1 Avoirdupois oz.	=	.911 Troy oz.
35.274 Avoirdupois oz.	=	1 kilogram

Sizes:

Inches	Millimeters
1/4	6.35
1/2	12.70
3/4	19.05
1	25.40
1¼	31.75
1½	38.10
1¾	44.45
2	50.08

DENOMINATIONS OF GOLD COINS

Amani — Afghanistan

Bahts — Thailand

Baiza — Muscat & Oman

Balboa — Panama

Centimes — Monaco

Colones — Costa Rica, Salvador
Centisimo — Uruguay

Condores — Chile

Cordoba — Nicaragua

Crown — Turks and Calicos Islands

Cruziero — Brazil

Dinar — Afghanistan, Bahrain, Iraq,
Jordan, Kuwait, Yugoslavia

Dollars — Anguilla, Bahamas, Belize,
Bermuda, Canada, Cayman Islands,
Cook Islands, Ethiopia, Fiji Islands,
Jamaica, Liberia, Singapore

Drachma — Greece

Ducat — Czechoslovakia, Liechtenstein,
Netherlands, Netherland East Indies

Emalangeni — Swaziland
Fil — Jordan

Florin — Hungary

Forint — Hungary

Franc — Albania, Burundi, Camaroon,
Central African Republic, Chad, Congo,
Dahomey, France, French Polynesia,
Gabon, Guinea, Ivory Coast, Katanga,
Luxembourg, Mali, Monaco, Morocco,
New Hebrides, Niger, Rwanda, Saarland,
Senegal, Switzerland, Tunis

Franken — Liechtenstein

Golde — Sierra Leone

Gourde — Haiti

Gram — Bolivia, Brazil

Guaranie — Paraguay

Hau — Tonga

Hercules — Tangier

Imadi — Yemen

Kip — Laos

Koula — Tonga

Kreugerrand — South Africa

Kroner — Iceland

Kuna — Croatia

Lei — Roumania

Lek — Albania

Leone — Sierra Leone

Leva — Bulgaria

Libra — Peru.

Lilangeni — Swaziland

Lire — Italy, Vatican City

Maloti — Lesotho

Mohar — Nepal

Mohur — India

Pahlevi — Persia (Iran)

Peso — Central American Union, Chile,
Colombia, Dominican Republic, Mexico,
Uruguay

Peseta — Equatorial Guinea, Spain

Piastre — Egypt, Turkey

Piso — Phillipines

Pound — Biafra, Egypt, Falkland Islands,
Ghana, Great Britain, Isle of Man, Israel,
Jersey, Malta, Rhodesia, Saudi Arabia,
South Africa, Syria, United States of
America

Puffin — Lundy Island

Rand — South Africa

Riel — Cambodia

Ringgit — Malaysia

Riyals (Ryals) Ajman, Fujairah, Muscat &
Oman, Oman, Persia (Iran), Sharjah, Um
Al Qawain, Yemen

Rupee — Burma, Mauritius

Rupiah — Indonesia

Schilling — Austria

Sertum — Bhutan

Shillings — Kenya, Somalia, Tanzania,
Uganda

Sole — Peru

Thebe — Botswana

Tical — Thailand

Won — South Korea

Yuan — China

ADDENDUM

At publishing time the following items became available and could not be placed in logical sequence, and therefore appear here for your information.

CHINA

4. 2000 Yuan **$650**

Struck to commemorate the 50th Anniversary of the Founding of the Republic of China. Obv: Legend and Bust of Chang Ki Shek. Rev: Geometric Pattern. Weight 28 gms, size 33.33 mm. Mintage: unknown.

GERMANY

Unofficial gold 20 Mark pieces, struck privately, appeared on the market allegedly struck from original dies.

GREAT BRITAIN

Minted sovereigns dated 1974 same size, weight and design as prior Elizabeth II issue.

ISRAEL

Announced plans for a gold coin to commemorate the United States Bicentennial to be issued late 1975.

JORDAN

5. 100 Fils . . . . **est. $800**

Gold presentation piece exactly same as FAO Nickel Silver Coin Weight gms; size mm. Estimated 10-20 mintage.

RHODESIA

Photo of 5 Pound 1966

About the Author

Sanford J. Durst, a coin collector for many years, is a member of the New York State Bar. Prior to becoming an attorney, he graduated from Polytechnic Institute of New York as a Chemical Engineer, and is now a member of its Alumni Association Board of Trustees. Mr. Durst is also active as a commercial realtor, and is well known in this field in the New York area. He is a member of the Faculty of the City University of New York.

Notes

Notes

Notes

Notes

Notes

Notes

Notes

Notes

Notes

Notes

Notes

Notes

Notes

Notes

THE GOLD COIN NEWSLETTER

The exciting New Modern Gold Coin collecting investment hobby has been launched.

Important News and details in the field, immediately upon happening, is a must for you.

The GOLD COIN NEWSLETTER is designed for specifically that purpose. It will appear in a regular monthly issue, with flash announcements airmailed to you between regular Newsletters, as conditions dictate.

Included will be such urgent information as full details on:

1. New Issues, and where to order them.
2. Laws relating to ownership and importation of coins.
3. Tax Consequences of Gold ownership
4. Tips on Reselling coins for maximum profits.
5. Storage and Shipment of Coins.
6. Insurance of Coins.
7. The Bullion Coins Market—Analysis & Considerations.
8. Books and Literature available on Gold ownership.
9. Revised values of previously minted Gold coins on the U.S. and foreign market place.
10. Gold Coin Sleepers, prior to 1934.
11. Estates with Gold coins—problems and benefits.
12. How to deal with overseas firms, and the pitfalls in doing so.
13. U.S. and Foreign Banks in the Gold Business.
14. Counterfeit information

plus many, many other relevant ideas and pieces of information aimed at enriching your knowledge, collection and net worth.

The Newsletter service should more than pay for itself with just one bit of information you use.

The price: $18.00/year postpaid, Airmail, USA and Canada; $22.00/year postpaid overseas. Foreign Subscribers, kindly remit in US dollars payable on a US Bank, if possible.

Mail your application today to:

The Gold Coin Newsletter
c/o Sanford J. Durst
133 East 58th Street
New York, New York 10022